Praise for
Retire Often

"*Retire Often* provides a roadmap for ambitious professionals to accelerate their careers—without working nonstop! Sabbatical programs aren't talked about enough, and Jillian Johnsrud is starting an important conversation."

—**Jason Feifer, Editor in Chief, *Entrepreneur* Magazine**

"Sometimes it feels like we have to choose between financial freedom and a life of adventure. Jillian shows us it's possible to have both. *Retire Often* offers keen insights and fresh perspectives that will help anyone navigate their life's path with confidence."

—**Ryan Nicodemus, Co-founder of The Minimalists**

"Most of us face a false choice: work until we're ready to retire forever, as though retirement is a one-way door. But there's a smarter path. Mini-retirements let you strategically hit pause, realign your priorities, and enjoy epic adventures punctuated throughout your life. *Retire Often* delivers the practical blueprint for how to do this—without blowing up your finances or career momentum. The key takeaway? Retirement isn't an all-or-nothing proposition. You can experience multiple meaningful breaks throughout your journey while also building long-term wealth."

—**Paula Pant, Host of the Afford Anything podcast**

"*Retire Often* will give you a vision for how you can design your working career and finances in an entirely different way; one that reflects your values and gives space for your biggest goals."

—**Joshua Becker, Founder of Becoming Minimalist and Author of *Things That Matter***

From People Who've Taken Mini-retirements

"I wish I had this book earlier in my life as it would have helped me transition into retirement had I done a few mini-retirements first. My favorite quote is 'Without a plan, you'll miss 50% of the benefits a mini-retirement can offer' which makes sense for retirement too. Had I done some of the work suggested in this book—I could have saved a year and a half of regretting my decision and second-guessing myself."

—**Darlene Deane, took a seven-month mini-retirement**

"The concept of seasons and reminder that certain ideas have expiration dates was powerful for me when planning my own mini-retirement. Whether you are dreaming about what a break may look like or you are ready to take the leap, *Retire Often* provides a guide to help you think with intention to make the most of your time away. Pick up this book; it will show you the way."

—**Stacy Blackshear, took a 12-month mini-retirement**

"In *Retire Often* Jillian helps the reader create an actionable roadmap for a successful and life-renewing mini-retirement—a work pause to focus on family, friends, travel, life experiences, or simply just a break from life passing by. The thought-provoking exercises provide bite-sized action steps to answer your 'what, when, why and how' mini-retirement questions, including the all-important employer conversation. This book is for those looking to press a work pause on life's fast-forward button!"

—**Ed Tudino, mini-retirement test run became full retirement**

"As a career-focused individual who took a bold Family Gap Year with my husband, three kids, and our dog, *Retire Often* resonated deeply with me. It's a powerful guide for anyone considering a mini-retirement, offering practical advice on recovering from burnout, reigniting creativity, and crafting a meaningful story about your break. Chapter Six, in particular, provided actionable insights on how to turn a once-in-a-lifetime experience into a narrative that sets you apart, whether returning to work or starting fresh. This book is a must-read for anyone dreaming of stepping away from the grind to rediscover purpose and possibility."

—**Heidi Dusek, took a 18-month mini-retirement**

"The idea of taking a career break is an anxiety-inducing proposition for most high performers. *Retire Often* bridges the gap between the terrifying void in your imagination and creating the most fulfilling, transformational time of your life. With Jillian's clear guidance and coaching, your mini-retirement(s) will be well-planned, thoughtfully executed, and propel you to your next growth phase with confidence."

—**Laura Rojo-Eddy, currently on a 9+ month mini-retirement**

"Jillian possesses a remarkable talent for guiding you through each step to turn your dream of taking a work break into reality. She tackles concerns you might not even realize you'll face on your path to a mini-retirement. Most importantly, Jillian instills the confidence to embrace your boldest dreams. She did it for me, and with this book, I'm certain she'll do the same for you."

—Julia Anderson, currently on a 6+ month mini-retirement

"Thinking about taking a mini-retirement but don't know where to start? Jillian is like a supportive friend that lays out a solid, actionable roadmap to help you make it happen. It's the guide I wish my wife and I had when planning ours—it would've given us so much more clarity, confidence, and would've saved us so much money!"

—Joe Jimenez, 6+ mini-retirements completing six thru-hikes

RETIRE OFTEN

RETIRE OFTEN

How anyone can take multiple career breaks to unlock adventure, advance their career, and find financial freedom

JILLIAN JOHNSRUD

Harriman House

HARRIMAN HOUSE LTD
Website: harriman.house

First published in 2025 by Harriman House, an imprint of Pan Macmillan
Associated companies throughout the world
www.panmacmillan.com

Copyright © Jillian Johnsrud 2025

The right of Jillian Johnsrud to be identified as the author has been asserted in accordance with the Copyright, Design and Patents Act 1988.

Paperback ISBN: 978-1-80409-098-5
eBook ISBN: 978-1-80409-100-5

All rights reserved. No part of this publication may be reproduced, stored in a retrieval system, or transmitted in any form or by any means (including without limitation electronic, mechanical, photocopying, recording, or otherwise) without the prior written permission of the publisher. This book is sold subject to the condition that it shall not, by way of trade or otherwise, be lent, hired out, or otherwise circulated without the publisher's prior consent. This work is reserved from text and data mining (Article 4(3) Directive (EU) 2019/790).

Harriman House does not have any control over, or any responsibility for, any author or third-party websites (including without limitation URLs, emails and QR codes) referred to in or on this book. This book is for informational purposes only. Readers are advised to consult an appropriate professional in light of their relevant circumstances and requirements before acting on any information in this book.

No responsibility or liability for loss occasioned to any person or corporate body acting or refraining to act as a result of reading material in this book can be accepted by the publisher, by the author, or by the employers of the author.

01

Printed in the United States of America.

To Adam, the relentless supporter of my dreams.

CONTENTS

Foreword by JL Collins	xiii
About the Author	xvii
Introduction: Small Career Breaks for a Bigger Life	1
Step One: From Dreams to Plans	15
Chapter One: The Secret Blend for Mini-Retirement Success	17
Chapter Two: Three Tools to Design a Life-changing Mini-Retirement	39
Chapter Three: Choosing Your Next Adventure	51
Chapter Four: Recover from Burnout	63
Step Two: Unexpected Career Benefits	73
Chapter Five: Uplevel your Career	75
Chapter Six: Crafting Your Mini-Retirement Story	81
Chapter Seven: Negotiate Your Sabbatical	91
Chapter Eight: Exit Negotiation	105
Chapter Nine: Negotiate the Unusual	111
Chapter Ten: Before You Go, and Finding the Next Job	119
Chapter Eleven: Self-Employed	131
Chapter Twelve: Call Me Crazy	141
Chapter Thirteen: Pack Your Mini-Retirement Go Bag	153

Step Three: Figure Out the Finances   159

    Chapter Fourteen: A Mini-Retirement to Improve Your Finances   161

    Chapter Fifteen: Finding Your Baseline Budget   167

    Chapter Sixteen: Build Your Dream Budget   177

    Chapter Seventeen: 6.5% for a Lifetime of Mini-Retirements   185

    Chapter Eighteen: Old Age and In Between   197

    Chapter Nineteen: Fill the Five Buckets   205

    Chapter Twenty: Healthcare (in the U.S.)   217

Step Four: Navigating the Mini-Retirement Journey   229

    Chapter Twenty-one: Prepare for the Unexpected   231

Acknowledgments   263

Let's Connect   267

FOREWORD BY JL COLLINS

YOU DON'T *NEED* TO READ THIS BOOK. The title should be enough to put the idea of mini-retirements in your head. I didn't even have that back in the day, yet this is how I handled my career. I retired often, although I wasn't smart enough to think of it in those terms.

For the most part, I loved working. I just didn't want to do it all the time. So whenever I felt the need, I stepped away. Sometimes for a few months. Once for five years. Mostly it was my call, but there was that time my company kicked me to the curb and there I was.

But you *should* read this book, and boy howdy how I wish I'd had it back then. If I had, my mini-retirements (which, make no mistake, were great) could have been so much better. So much less stressful. So much more beneficial. Instead of wandering in the wilderness feeling lost, I would have had this map. I would have had Jillian at my metaphorical side, guiding and reassuring me as I made my way. But I didn't. She hadn't written this book yet. But now she has, and now she is here for you.

In these pages Jillian shares with us exactly how to do it. How to minimize the risk and maximize the benefits, and how to create a whole new world of experiences. My wilderness wandering was wonderful, and I am so glad I did it. But now *Retire Often* has blazed the trail, shows us where the quicksand lurks, and takes us to all the scenic overlooks, many of which I simply didn't know were there.

For one thing, I would have better understood and more easily accepted the mixed emotions triggered by stepping away. The good, the bad, and the baffling. Make no mistake, taking mini-retirements is an exhilarating experience, but those emotions definitely can present challenges along with the thrills.

Learning how to recover from a stressful job with active rest and "un-rushing" (a concept I love!), and how to keep off the couch and free of the mind-numbing TV trap, are worth the read alone. But there is so much more.

Jillian lays out four steps:

- From Dreams to Plans
- Unexpected Career Benefits
- Figure Out the Finances
- Navigating the Mini-retirement Journey

In the first three, she shows us how to plan our journey, gear up, pack our knapsacks and bravely set out into our adventure. Step four is all about your compass and navigating your way into this undiscovered country.

For me, step three was always my strong suit. Investing and finance are in my wheelhouse. But looking back, the others were not.

Sadly, I never really did much dreaming or planning around my mini-retirements. Mostly I waited till I was burning out and then just pulled the trigger. Figuring out what came next, well, came next. While this mostly worked out, it didn't always. But either way, as I read, I couldn't help but wonder how much better each journey would have been with the kind of forethought in these pages. Being aware of what Jillian calls our "seasons of life" and, critically, that these carry expiration dates, would have made a huge difference in my approach.

Each time I did this it felt like I was putting my career in danger. The idea that there could actually be career benefits was stunning to me. Maybe it shouldn't have been such an eyeopener. Looking back, stepping away never seemed to hurt my work or career. But it always felt like a risk and, while I was certainly willing to take it, the sense of unease was ever present.

Had I read *Retire Often*, I would have known about the almost magical force that helps pull you back into the workforce when you are ready (and sometimes before you are), and I would have learned how playing it well can propel you into even stronger and more lucrative positions.

Step Two would have made me far more effective in negotiating my departures and returns, opening up whole new potential avenues I never considered. It also would have made me better at crafting the stories around my taking this unconventional step, making employers more comfortable with and open to my eventual return. For example, here are two rules regarding creating stories I especially loved:

Rule One: Everything must be true.
Rule Two: It can't be the whole truth.

If these seem obvious, the details may surprise you.

Back in the day, I didn't really bother with or even think about the guidance Jillian offers in Step Four. I simply had no awareness. But my journey would have been considerably more psychologically comfortable and understandable for me, and those around me, if I had.

But that's me. You are very likely different. Maybe for you the career benefits are glaringly obvious and it is the financial advice in Step Three that paves your way. Perhaps the whole idea will come as a revelation and Step One will open the floodgates of your dreams. Or some other combination. Maybe this whole concept and approach is going to be like walking out of a dense, damp fog into the bright warm sunlight.

Regardless, I'll wager you'll be glad you picked up this book. Your life, your career, and your many coming retirements will be lastingly richer for it.

JL Collins
Author of *The Simple Path to Wealth* and *Pathfinders*

ABOUT THE AUTHOR

JILLIAN JOHNSRUD never expected to be able to retire early, so she hatched a plan to retire often. Inspired by the idea of sabbatical years, she set out to sprinkle retirements throughout her and Adam's working lives. At 40, they have taken over a dozen mini-retirements. These allowed them to pursue dreams like living abroad,

traveling to 27 countries, adopting four kids (plus two biological kids), investing in real estate, and touring the U.S. in a camper.

Jillian has taught, coached, and wrote about mini-retirements for almost a decade. She hosts the *Retire Often* podcast and is a popular speaker and consultant for mini-retirements. She lives in Montana, where she spends time in the garden drinking tea.

INTRODUCTION: SMALL CAREER BREAKS FOR A BIGGER LIFE

MY HUSBAND, ADAM, and I were driving through the vineyards and orchards of southern Idaho when we stumbled on the question that changed everything.

Newly married and still in college, we often had long conversations, dreaming about what this new life together would look like. I had been reading through the Old Testament (as the young kids do) and came across the idea of a sabbatical year.

"I've been learning," I said, suddenly excited, "that in the ancient world, every seven years, everyone took the whole year off. It's an incredible idea."

"Yeah, I guess," he replied, a little confused.

"Well," I continued, "what if we did that?"

He tilted his head the way a perplexed dog would. "Did what? A sabbatical?"

"Yeah, it could be amazing. Every seven years, we take a whole year off. We would only have to set aside an extra 10 or 15% a year to cover our costs. Think about all the cool things we could do with that year!"

There was a long pause. And then a slow, drawn-out response. "Um, honey, I'm not sure people do that anymore. I'm not even sure if they did that back then. It is a cool idea. But I don't know how we would pull that off."

I responded with the question I've now said a hundred times since then: **"But what if we could?"**

The question that changed everything.

My imagination was on fire with all the possibilities. Maybe instead of working for the next 40 years straight and retiring for 20 years after that, we could sprinkle in smaller mini-retirements. We could fill our life with adventures and tackle our biggest goals.

Of course, there were lots of things to consider. What about healthcare? How would we find a job when we were done? What would we even *do* during that year? Could we really afford to save an extra 10%? We still had student loans!

I didn't have all the answers. Or really *any* answers to those questions. I just had a little dream. A vision of what our life could look like if we stepped away from the 9–5 to focus on other things that mattered to us.

Rather than one massive retirement, could we retire often?

WHAT IS A MINI-RETIREMENT?

Mini-retirements go by many names: sabbatical, gap year, hiatus, career break. There is so much crossover in meaning that you can use the labels almost interchangeably. I'm not sure there is an official definition, but there is a structure I've seen that is most effective.

Here are the three elements necessary to experience a mini-retirement.

INTRODUCTION

A mini-retirement is any time you:

1. step away from your primary career
2. for a month or longer
3. to focus on things that matter to you.

It's that simple.

When you think about it that way, you will probably have an opportunity to experience a mini-retirement. With some preparation, you can take advantage of natural career breaks. You could utilize a few months after college before your first job. Maybe you move across the country and take a month or two off. You might be laid off, and it could require a few months to find work. If you decide to have children, you might spend a few months or years away from your career.

Retiring often is about maximizing the benefit of these mini-retirements—and, with a small amount of intention and preparation, being able to take **many more mini-retirements**.

Let's look at those three elements one at a time.

1. Stepping away from your primary career

There are two main ways people step away from their career, which we will cover in Step Two of this book.

For shorter mini-retirements, one to three months, you might be able to negotiate the time off with your employer.

Longer mini-retirements, like six to twelve months, fit nicely between jobs.

For most people, a mini-retirement will involve no work at all. Life will be full of new things like travel, dinner parties, art classes, or hiking. While others explore passions, expand hobbies, take on side hustles, or finally start that business they have been dreaming of.

Most likely, there will be no paid work during your mini-retirement. But there may be ways to use your time off to improve your finances or career. During one of our mini-retirements, Adam and I bought a rental house and remodeled it for a month. Now, construction work might sound worse than your regular job. But in that season of life, he had an extremely stressful job doing case management for kids in a group home, similar to a child protective worker. Every day was filled with high-stakes emergencies. So, for a month, we hung cabinets and painted walls. Painting is simple and easy; best of all, it stays done.

2. For a month or longer

Why is a month or more considered the benchmark for mini-retirement? A week-long vacation is nice. A two-week vacation can be amazing. But things really start to shift in week three or four. Your body and mind begin to relax at a deeper level. You start to disconnect from work mentally.

A month, well planned, is also enough time to do something significant. You could tackle a big project like a kitchen remodel, decluttering your house, touring with a band, or writing the first draft of your book. A month is long enough for a big adventure. For one mini-retirement, my best friend and I road-tripped from D.C. to Seattle and back. It was an incredible and transformative experience. Once, Adam and I traveled with our five kids in a pop-up camper around the country to visit extended family for six weeks. In both cases, I felt satisfied by the end. The trip was like finishing a good meal. I thoroughly enjoyed it but wasn't hungry for more.

Your options and opportunities only expand from there. If you can take three to six months or even a year or two, fantastic. But never discount a well-planned month.

3. To focus on things that matter to you

Time with people you love. Adventure. Recovery from burnout. Hobbies. Travel. The list of ways to make this time meaningful is endless. The key is to be intentional. In Step One, you'll learn how to create the three mini-retirement phases.

> If you find yourself suddenly unemployed, it can be easy to swim in shame and frustration while you binge Netflix for a month. That's not a mini-retirement; that's low-key despair. Your mini-retirement might have a few purposes and goals. The key is finding things that really matter to you. One of the quickest ways to waste a mini-retirement is having no plan.

You might think, *"My job is so awful; as long as I'm not there, life will be great."* So you don't plan or prepare any way to make the time meaningful. Happiness is one part reducing suffering, and one part adding meaning and joy. Time away from work isn't enough. Without a plan, you'll miss 50% of the benefits a mini-retirement can offer. The next chapter will explore the top ten ways people use a mini-retirement, focusing on two themes: "seasons with expiration dates" and "things that don't fit into nights and weekends."

LIFE-CHANGING: PERSONALLY, PROFESSIONALLY, FINANCIALLY

Taking a dozen mini-retirements over the last 20 years has transformed every area of my life. Each one created a shift in my trajectory. The most obvious question is on the personal side. I have been able to travel to 27 countries, adopt four kids, improve my mental health, have time with friends and family, and pursue hobbies like planting a food forest and learning tango.

How mini-retirements improve your career and finances seems counterintuitive. Professionally and financially, you are removing a known thing (work) and replacing it with an unknown thing.

You are replacing your time at work with a *possibility*. I know how scary that is. But also how exciting.

If you return to work less burned out, you could *possibly* get a promotion. If you take a year to buy a rental or start a side gig, you could *possibly* increase your income long term. When you get your next job, it could *possibly* come with a 20% raise. It's easier to calculate the downside than to anticipate the potential upside. That doesn't mean there isn't an upside. *Possibly* a significant upside for your career and finances.

Suppose you storm out of your office tomorrow without notice and buy a one-way ticket to Europe. In that case, your mini-retirement might be a wash or even a detriment. Having helped craft hundreds of mini-retirement plans, stick with me in this process, follow my four steps, and be smart with your plan. No matter your professional or financial starting point, you could make huge gains.

The system is broken. Be a kid for five years. Train for your job for 12–20 years. Work your job for 40 years. Then, if you are lucky and still healthy, you get to fit in all the things you missed out on. There are some obvious flaws to this plan.

The old system says, *"Be as happy and fulfilled as possible with your nights and weekends. Try not to be disappointed or frustrated by that. Because, at 65, you can attempt to squeeze in everything you have missed out on during the first six decades of your life."*

INTRODUCTION

Personally: Build your best life now

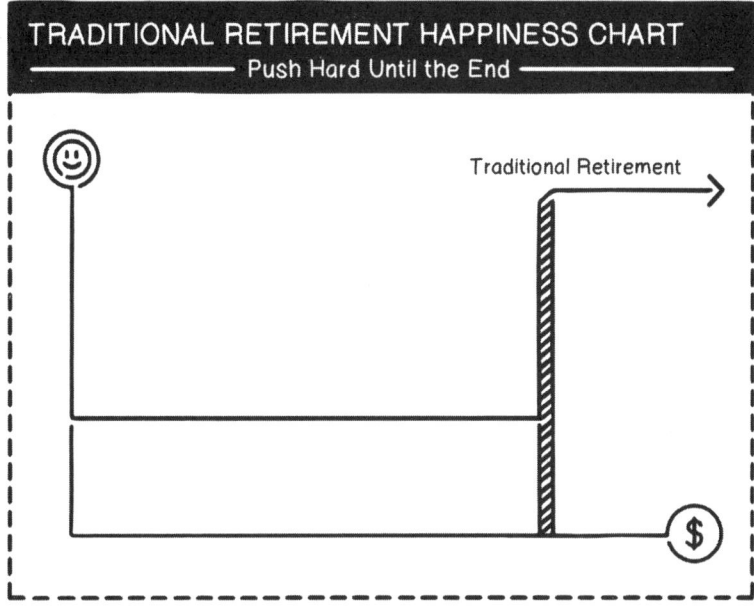

At some point in life, you'll be financially independent (FI), meaning your assets and/or social security can cover all your bills indefinitely. Maybe this happens at 70 or 55 or 35. No matter the age you can retire, the mistake people make is waiting until they are financially independent to start practicing this FI lifestyle.

What if you sprinkle in these mini-retirements throughout your working life? Each time, you tackle some of the changes you want to make. You practice some new habits. You could take up running or learn to meditate. You use the time to focus on personal growth and improving communication skills. You engage in new hobbies or dive deeper into old hobbies.

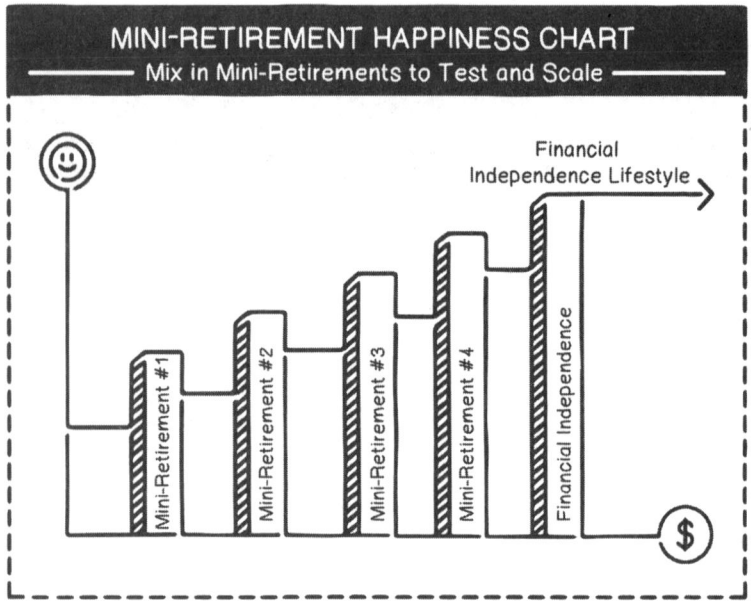

After each mini-retirement, you can maintain some of the changes. Your new yoga habit may stick around. You learned how to better communicate with your spouse. You have restored a classic car and now can enjoy that hobby more on the weekends. You were able to get involved in a non-profit and currently serve on the board, which you can maintain while you work your job because it only requires six hours a year. Each mini-retirement increases your happiness. And the next one builds from there.

While some people dream of retirement, hoping it will solve all their woes, others are fearful of the idea. *"I could never retire! I don't know what I would do with myself. I would be so bored. I can't just sit around all day."* And I get it. Most people *can't* just sit around all day. That does sound boring.

Finding ways to organize your time, develop hobbies, and find meaning and purpose outside of your work is a learning curve. For most of your life, someone else told you how to organize your time and defined success, first at school, then at a job. They gave you clear goals, rewarded you with incentives, and let you know where to be, what to focus on, and how much time it should take. In retirement, no one will create the structure or write the rules for you. It's up to you. And you might not have any practice. Creating a life you love takes time, intention, and experimentation. You have to figure out what brings you joy. You need to invest in relationships. You discover the thing that creates a sense of progress.

Professionally: How career breaks elevate your trajectory

There is a fear that taking short career breaks will be detrimental to a person's professional growth. Time and again, I've seen the opposite. Short, well-timed career breaks catapult people ahead professionally, significantly elevating their trajectory. From CEOs to hourly employees, their mini-retirement helped them leapfrog their burned-out and overwhelmed peers.

I grew up in a small wheat and cattle town in Montana. Hard work sewed the fabric of the community together. After the late summer harvest, all attention turned to high school football and women's basketball. In fourth grade, I prayed for three things each night before I went to sleep; one of those was to be tall. My dream was to be part of that basketball team. The fact I barely had talent didn't deter me, not even a little bit.

If you have ever watched or played sports, half-times are critical. This is where you, as an individual and as a team, regroup, refocus, and rest. It's a short pause to help you reimagine the rest of the game. No one opts out of the half-time.

A **career break is a half-time.** It allows you to regroup, refocus, and rest. It's a quick breather so you can finish the game strong. The best players use half-times. The most dedicated players use them. The hardest-working players use them. A mini-retirement is no different.

To expand this metaphor, if a one-to-three month mini-retirement is a half-time where you take leave from a current employer then return to the same job, then three to 12 months off between jobs is the time between games. I've played back-to-back games during tournaments, and with each game performance declines. Without breaks, people get sluggish, make simple mistakes, and morale tanks. Longer breaks between games is how players stay fresh, sharp, and full of hustle. A short career break between jobs refreshes you before you dive into the next job.

This is the workflow of most elite athletes, people literally at the top of their game. Taking a break doesn't mean they are weak, broken, or apathetic. That's an old stereotype that companies are quickly disregarding. Many entrepreneurs leading the way in innovation are starting to take four to six weeks off every year.

When being the best matters, this is one tool to get there. Here are five ways a career break can give you a professional boost.

1. **Improved performance**: Working in commissioned sales, I saw our best salespeople's performance numbers drop by 50% whenever they were dealing with a crisis at home. Their client interactions were only slightly different, but if they were going through a divorce or death in the family, the sales numbers tanked. It's easy to fool yourself (and others) that you are running at 100%. But even if you can give 80%, you might have disproportionately worse results. If a runner can only perform at 80%, she doesn't lose 20% of her races, she loses all of them. When people return to work, their performance improves. They are playing the game at a new level, and that gets noticed. The productivity boost and increased performance might be the difference in receiving a promotion, larger bonus, or raise.

2. **Additional training**: Your next promotion or next amazing job might be dependent on a class or certification. Mini-retirements help level the playing field for people who don't have the ability to complete those alongside their full-time jobs. Or it might be the chance to improve certain skills like presenting, conflict resolution, or communication. Even if you're excellent at 90% of your job, there might be one missing skill set that could hamper your career growth for decades.
3. **New opportunity**: After a client of mine submitted his notice, heads of other departments started to scramble to set up lunches with him before he left. *"Might you be interested in working in their department? There is a role that could be perfect!"* No one had ever approached him about these opportunities before. Stepping away from work puts you top of mind. In Step Two, we'll explore how to leverage this even further.
4. **Pay bump with new job**: Switching companies is the best way to get a significant raise. If you take a six-month mini-retirement but land a job with a 20% pay increase, your mini-retirement is paid for in a few years. Now, you have increased your lifetime earnings substantially.
5. **Career pivot**: Many people use mini-retirements to reimagine their next chapter professionally. This can improve your finances in two ways: You could earn more per year in your new career, or decide you want to work longer. Instead of a job you are trying to escape at 50 for fear that to work any longer you might die at your desk, you might find something you'll love doing at 70.

Knowing some of these benefits, many companies have tried unlimited paid time off (PTO). While a week's vacation is great, the magic happens in about a month. Most employees feel uncomfortable or nervous about pushing it too far without a clear expectation of what unlimited PTO means. When other people are picking up your work and covering for you, there can be some guilt on an extended vacation. If no one is covering your work, you return to double work, which discourages taking any vacation at all.

Financially: Time away, and richer for it

Counterintuitive, isn't it? How does taking time away (earning less) and doing something meaningful (potentially spending more) equal being richer?

Being successful in your personal finances is one part motivation and one part knowledge. Your mini-retirement will be the perfect motivation to master the six financial pillars that we will cover in Step Three.

1. **Track your expenses**: You'll learn how to observe your spending (free of judgment or shape), then improve your financial choices moving forward.
2. **Spend more intentionally**: By aligning your spending to your values and focusing on joy now and during your mini-retirement.
3. **Learn to budget and create financial plans**: You'll create your mini-retirement budget while learning how to budget your monthly expenses.
4. **Grow the gap**: By some combination of increasing income or reducing expenses, you'll grow the gap between your income and expenses.
5. **Guard the gap**: Make bigger money moves like investing, creating passive income or paying down debt to fund a lifetime of mini-retirements, with the five bucket approach.
6. **Financial empowerment**: After you learn to master these financial pillars and take your first mini-retirement, you'll see the incredible amount of agency you have over your financial life. Money isn't something that happens to you. You create the financial plans, and you make them happen.

INTRODUCTION

If you follow the four steps and retire often, you can experience incredible transformations in your personal life, career, and finances. When people take their first mini-retirement, at least one of these three areas improves significantly.

FOUR STEPS

There are only four steps to maximize the benefit of your next mini-retirement. While the steps aren't complicated, they are essential. Every time I hear about a lackluster mini-retirement, one or two steps were skipped entirely. A mini-retirement is too big a commitment of time and money to wing it.

In **Step One**, you will start to dream and plan what you could do with a month or a year off. I'll give you lots of tools to help you brainstorm and imagine what this time away from the 9–5 could look like. We will focus on what matters most to you and what makes sense in this season of life.

For **Step Two**, we will tackle the issue of your employment. This is exciting because you probably have more power and flexibility than you think. You'll learn how to successfully negotiate a mini-retirement from your employer. If you plan a longer mini-retirement, you'll be equipped with networking strategies to find an even better job.

Then, in **Step Three**, we will look at how to determine the budget for this mini-retirement. I'll also show you how to fill up the five buckets you can use to fund this mini-retirement and many more. Of course, I'll cover healthcare here as well. Especially for Americans, this is the logistical element that sends people into a tizzy.

After you have planned how you'll spend your time, worked it out with your employer, and saved the money, you will start

Step Four. This will be your road map so you'll know exactly what to expect, ways to optimize your time off, and how to overcome common challenges.

In the 22 years since that first conversation, Adam and I have taken over a dozen mini-retirements. I've helped hundreds of people successfully take life-changing mini-retirements. I wasn't sure what the answers to Adam's initial concerns were then, but I do now. That's what lies in the pages ahead. Everything you need to know to take your next mini-retirement and set yourself up for a lifetime of adventures.

There are so many beautiful things to experience in each season of life. It's not enough to retire once; you need to retire often.

STEP ONE

FROM DREAMS TO PLANS

CHAPTER ONE

THE SECRET BLEND FOR MINI-RETIREMENT SUCCESS

A DAM'S PANDEMIC HOBBY was learning to cook Thai food. A pursuit I highly encouraged! Having only been an enjoyer of Thai food, not a creator, he started by finding recipes online. We quickly learned that the right balance of flavors is a delicate yet critical thing, when the first few batches ended up in the trash can with just a few too many hot peppers.

Just like a recipe, having a well-crafted plan for your mini-retirement is essential if you want a good outcome. Sweating and eyes watering aren't good looks during dinner or a mini-retirement.

Step One is all about crafting a highly effective mini-retirement plan. Before we dive into the specifics of what your time off will look like, you first need to choose your focus. Big picture, what do you want to get out of this career break? What's your intention? What would you love to see accomplished by the end of your mini-retirement?

In this chapter, I'll highlight the top ten ways people use their mini-retirements. None of them are (or need be) stand-alone. Imagine each of these ten areas of focus are ingredients, each adding a flavor to your career break. What three ingredients work well together? By combining a few areas of focus and making it multifunctional, you can maximize the value of your time away. As you read through these top ten, see what resonates with you. Do any of these stories or ideas spark some inspiration?

Some ingredients don't mix as well as others. If you try to combine them, it makes the whole dish taste worse. We'll get into what to avoid soon.

While focusing on all ten goals can be tempting, I urge restraint.

Here are two filters that can help you select the two or three goals that makes the most sense for your next mini-retirement. Retiring often means you don't have to do everything all at once; there will be many opportunities to add these things to your life.

FILTER 1. SEASONS IN LIFE WITH EXPIRATION DATES

While camping in Oregon during one of our mini-retirements, I met a couple in their 60s who had just begun hiking the Pacific Crest Trail, a hike spanning 2,600 miles along the West Coast. They were only at the start but seemed discouraged already. (Newly acquired blisters might have contributed to their mood.) My family and I were in the middle of a big trip as well.

Usually, when we traveled with all five kids in our pop-up camper, I felt like a great adventurer. But I was outdone by the gumption of these two. I made them coffee before they departed for the day's hike, and chatted about the motivations for taking this trip. They weren't retired yet but worried they couldn't postpone another five years. In fact, they wondered if they had already waited too long.

After finishing the coffee, the man said, "We'll do our best and see how far we make it. But I know we wouldn't make it further if we waited longer to try."

If we are honest with ourselves, some things in life don't have a five- or ten-year shelf life. They have to be done when they have to be done. Or there'll be no doing them. Seasons in life have an expiration date.

Maybe your parents or grandparents are getting older, and they want to hike through Scotland before all the cartilage in their knees is gone. Maybe your kids are still young enough to love a road trip and not bemoan missing Wi-Fi and friends. Suppose a health diagnosis becomes a limiting factor in the future. If you wait ten years, the window will have closed.

One of my early mini-retirements was a coast-to-coast trip in my 20s with my best friend. We camped in national parks and slept on friends' couches. I'm so thankful I took that trip because it's not a trip I will ever replicate. For one thing, I don't sleep on the frozen ground anymore. I gave that up when I turned 30. That season has passed. My friend and I lived on instant oatmeal, microwave popcorn, and candy. Now my body requires vegetables. That month-long mini-retirement remains one of my favorites, not just because it was a healing balm for a challenging season in my life but because it won't happen again.

FILTER 2. GOALS THAT ARE CHALLENGING TO SQUEEZE INTO NIGHTS AND WEEKENDS

Even a week-long vacation isn't sufficient for some kinds of plans. You can't walk the Camino, take a cross-country road trip with your best friend, or recover from burnout in just seven days.

Then there are projects you can do at home—in theory, at any time. But fitting them alongside a busy job and all your other obligations takes energy and mental bandwidth. I took one summer off and planted a food forest in my backyard. I transformed my yard with a gazebo, flagstone patio, 20 fruit trees, dozens of berry bushes, hundreds of flowers, and a few months of hard work. I could have chipped away at this project for a decade. But I wanted to eat fresh plums and pick currants in a few years, not a decade.

As you read through these ten focuses, jot down the two or three that really speak to you.

RETIRE OFTEN

TOP TEN FOCUSES FOR A MINI-RETIREMENT

1. Travel, travel, and more travel

Every week a promotional email arrives in my inbox full of travel deals. A three-night all-inclusive in Cabo, Mexico. A six-night tour through Italy, seeing three major cities. A four-day Caribbean cruise with two ports of call. Why take a mini-retirement to travel when these offers are at our fingertips?

On a mini-retirement, there are two types of travel that people crave, and they don't fit into a long weekend or limited vacation days.

Meaningful travel

I was sitting in a classroom that felt more like an attic of an historic building when the teacher greeted us, first in Italian, then in English. I'm not sure what prompted me to take a class titled "Expat Literature in Italy" in Rome. I hadn't read any literature since being assigned it in high school. But this was a season of life of trying new things and pushing myself out of my comfort zone.

I had taken these traveling classes before. They offered three credit hours but compressed them into ten-hour days for two weeks with a passionate teacher and about 15 classmates. This was my third one. "Scottish Poetry and History" took place in a large, castle-like manor in St. Andrews, Scotland. The Scottish owner reused every student's tea bag but didn't fail to mention that Prince William and his then-fiancée, Kate Middleton, had considered buying her home.

"Van Gogh's Life and Art" class took place at the Van Gogh Museum in Amsterdam. Time spent in class was brief, though. It was never long before the teacher sent us out on increasingly abstruse painting assignments. Each nonsensical prompt filled my perfectionist heart with fear-riddled anxiety. "Paint the shadows" wasn't enough instruction for me.

These classes allowed me to explore and enjoy travel in a whole new way. Travel creates an opportunity to learn, grow as a person, serve, or connect with a culture or a history in a more meaningful way. I've flown into Vegas for a few fun days with friends. It's nice. But for a mini-retirement, people often seek something weightier.

On my podcast, when I interview people about their mini-retirements, meaningful travel is a frequent theme. I talked to Chad about how he lived with his family for a year in Spain, working on his Spanish, which culminated in a long-held dream of being interviewed about personal finance for Spanish TV, entirely utilizing his Spanish. Rachel shared how she hiked the Camino as she gained the courage to start her own business. Angel explained how he traveled through Mexico with his new wife and baby to share his home country with them. Brooke's adventure was traveling solo through Southeast Asia after her divorce to gain confidence and reimagine what this next chapter of her life would be like. To acquaintances, these might have looked like fun trips. But for my podcast guests, the travel meant something more. Travel can be life-changing because you are changed in the process.

Slow travel

Have you ever come back from a vacation and felt like you needed a vacation from your vacation? With such limited time off, it's natural that we want to fit everything in. Because who knows if you'll ever be able to come back to this place? There's pressure to make the most of it.

Unfortunately, these trips start to feel a lot like life back home. Full. Busy. Overscheduled.

That's where slow travel—something only enabled by mini-retirements—comes in.

Every year, we take a big road trip with our kids. Sometimes for eight weeks, sometimes eight months. It surprises people to hear, but I don't plan many activities in advance. When you travel slowly, you realize there are interesting things everywhere. And once you've done all the "big things"—the best museums, the biggest zoos, the most impressive churches, and the iconic historical sites—you start to appreciate the small things. The weird things. The *"you won't find this anyplace else, because why would anyone else bother?"* things.

Those attractions have become my favorite. The petting zoo in a park in Amsterdam where we weren't allowed to pet the animals. The campground outside of Yosemite that had a petting zoo where you *could* pet all the animals, causing one of my kids to be nibbled on and Adam spat at by the llama. The Oregon Trail Museum in Wyoming, where we stopped due to bad weather. The little gelato shop along the Rhine River in Germany that serves a Riesling gelato.

Taking in the smaller and more textured parts of travel isn't the only benefit to slow travel. Familiar and friendly things are hard to come by with rapid travel schedules.

When your travel itinerary has five attractions today and a new city by tomorrow, something is lost. You give up the small joys. The café with your new favorite pastry, the marzipan twist you will think about a decade later. The friends your kids will make at the playground. The seldom-occupied park bench with the best view.

When you travel slow, you can return three, four or a dozen times until these small places start to feel comfortable and familiar, like a childhood memory. The "top ten" attractions are great, but these small places add color and warmth to your trip. When your friends ask about the highlights of your trip to Amsterdam, you know they want to hear about the Anne Frank House or the Van

Gogh Museum. But you kinda just want to talk about the petting zoo where you weren't allowed to pet the animals.

2. Quality time

While mini-retirements are wonderful for epic adventures, they can also give you more time with the people you love the most.

One summer, we had no big travel plans and instead decided to do "daily adventures." Every day, we did something fun out of the house. A trip to the park, getting an ice cream, relaxing at the lake, or a hike. We live in an amazing vacation destination but never had the chance to be hometown tourists.

In the most demanding seasons of our careers, it's easy to miss out on small moments of joy with the people we love. Just staying caught up at work, a clean house, and meals prepared feels like a huge victory. A mini-retirement can give you a margin for magic—the breathing room for unplanned get-togethers.

When my son was in kindergarten, I would arrive home from work 30 minutes before his bedtime. Because I worked retail, I had to work all day Saturday and half days Sunday. But early Saturday morning I would make us chocolate chip pancakes. It was one of the happiest moments of my week. Until work mandated an early Saturday meeting. I was devastated. Sometimes, the best and sweetest moments with the people we love are the simple ones. Stopping by my aunt's for a cup of tea or spending an hour in the garden with my dad.

I've been in that season of life where you schedule lunch with your friends eight weeks out. Adding more social obligations, well, feels like an obligation. Mini-retirements can bring back dinner parties, meet-ups with friends, play dates for your kids, and board games. You have more quantity of time, but you also have quality of time. You can give the people who love you the best version of yourself.

3. Extended family and friends

Your best friends from college post a photo of their four-year-old, and then the realization hits you: You haven't seen them in at least four years! How is that possible? Come to think of it, when did you last see your favorite cousins? I read a study that said the number of close friendships you maintain is a good predictor of lifespan. Not having many friends is just as impactful on your long-term health as being overweight, not exercising or even smoking.*

The modern career sets us up for failure and apparently a shorter life. The math simply doesn't work. Let's say you get 14 days of vacation a year. If you're married, you have your parents and your spouse's parents to visit. Add in siblings, a few close cousins, maybe an aunt or uncle you like. There are weddings if you are in your 20s and 30s, maybe school extracurriculars if you are in your 40s. Friends from college, a few childhood friends if you're lucky. Plus, on holidays you have to travel, eating up a few extra days. Heaven forbid you want an actual vacation. How do you spread 14 days over all those people? And if you can't figure out this wizardry, the consequence is early death!

At some point in our 30s or 40s, we realize that life isn't like a beer commercial with big groups of friends having a bonfire on the beach and tossing a frisbee. Maintaining all those connections after we move out of our childhood home and leave school requires time and energy. In the most demanding season of our career, it's easy to

---

* www.inc.com/jeff-haden/this-study-of-300000-people-reveals-1-secret-to-living-a-longer-healthier-life.html

let those connections go. Having more time with extended friends and family is therefore a great way to spend a mini-retirement.

A guest on my podcast shared how a week of his mini-retirement was spent with friends from college. Over the past ten years, they have got together three times. While he loved the trip and was able to be fully present and relaxed, a few of his friends had work issues come up, and instead of kayaking on the river they spent most of the time on their laptops in the cabin.

If you want to be able to visit friends and family that don't live down the street, you need more than 14 days. Mini-retirements made that possible for us. Every week during our road trip mini-retirements, we visit friends or family. Our family is spread out all over the country, and we shape our itinerary around that. We have friends from college, the military, entrepreneurship, and my coaching clients (now friends), scattered across the U.S. Maintaining relationships doesn't stress me out like it used to. With mini-retirements, the math finally works, and there is time to invest in all the people you care about.

4. Projects

The laundry room in our basement had that damp, dank sort of vibe to it, with cinderblock walls that wept when it rained and a cement floor that never seemed entirely clean. Wrapping the walls on two sides, we installed large metal shelves to help store all the items that might have gone in a garage if we had one.

Soon, the shelves were full, and we started placing things in front of the shelf. A cooler. A toolbox. A box of winter coats for the kids and a few sleds. That season of our life was so busy that this pile became the physical embodiment of our emotional state. More things piled on until a small avalanche impeded the dryer door.

This stuff landslide wasn't the only space in our home that

needed some attention. But we had no time or energy to tackle this daunting task.

Projects are lurking. Not tiny projects. Not the ones that can be wrapped up in 15 minutes. Instead, the projects that you need to block off some time for. Ideally, you aren't wiped out and overwhelmed when you start because these projects require some gumption to get going.

It might be a house project like remodeling a bathroom or repainting the living room. Maybe you want to redo some landscaping. There are large, nagging personal projects as well, like getting around to finishing your will or shopping for new insurance quotes.

During one mini-retirement, we decluttered our entire home and got rid of 50% of our stuff. Decluttering is a perfect mini-retirement project because it's a bear of a task. But it also makes your life easier, lighter, and simpler, with long-lasting benefits. Decluttering is incredibly hard to do the first time, but after you go back to work, rather easy to maintain.

With seven people in 1,700 sq ft, we had enough space for our people, but not nearly enough to be a storage unit for barely used items. Everything we owned needed to be hard-working. No lazy stuff allowed that could stretch out on a shelf for nine or 12 months with no job to do. Decluttering massively improved our quality of life and even our relationship with our kids. But it wasn't easy. Not only did it require way more time than one might expect, but it had a high emotional cost as well. Going through sentimental items, items that represented dreams not fulfilled or interests no longer pursued, wasn't a task to tackle at 9 p.m. after a grueling day of work.

CHAPTER ONE

Get caught up

So many of us feel behind, especially on everything that isn't urgent but is important. There is a pile of mail on the counter, you need to update online passwords, the car needs an oil change, and a cavity needs to be fixed.

Between work, family, and commitments, some things sit on the to-do list... indefinitely. All these things act like open tabs on your phone or computer. Each one left open isn't a big deal, but when there are 100 open tabs, it creates a mental burden that we carry through our days.

In addition to big projects, mini-retirements allow you to get caught up in life. Slowly but surely, you will close the tabs and experience more bandwidth to think clearly. When you return to work, you can enjoy your weekends guilt-free instead of buried under a to-do list.

5. Recover from burnout

Can you heal in the place that made you sick? Let's say your home has black mold. Can you get better while still living there? Probably, a little, if you take certain steps like opening the windows or running an air purifier or dehumidifier. Eighty-nine per cent of Americans say they have experienced burnout in the last year. Can you recover in the place that made you sick? Probably, a little.

While I get that your job wasn't designed with your purpose, family or health in mind, your job was at least designed to maximize your effectiveness and efficiency. Burnout causes less creativity, less productivity, and less problem-solving ability. This is endlessly frustrating and confusing for me. Why are 89% of employees in job roles that are making them worse at their jobs?

Living in Montana, one of my favorite activities is hiking along a mountain trail. If you walk slowly you can take it all in. The pine trees, birds chirping, a stream with brightly colored pebbles, and wildflowers. Your eyes can scan side to side, hoping to spot a deer or at least be mindful of the bears. The faster you walk, the more your eyes need to stay on the path. If you are trail running, you are forced to look at the next spot your feet will land, lest you trip on a rock or tree root. This is what burnout does to us. It narrows our vision. All we can focus on is the next step or two. It's survival mode.

If the reason you are running is because a bear is chasing you, you aren't taking in the flowers or the sound of the birds. You aren't pondering poetry or how to solve a complex work problem. All you can see is where to put your feet next.

With such a narrow vision, you miss out at work and in life. You can't think about the big picture, solve hard challenges, or pay attention to other team members.

I've seen people recover from burnout in real-time. Slowly, their vision widens. They can start to imagine what type of job they would like to do next. They are able to have fun with their family. Their creativity and intuition return. Energy, motivation, and enthusiasm bubble up. They start cooking healthy meals, calling their mom, and pitching more clients at work. Instead of being hyper-focused on survival, they can see the big picture in their career, finances, family, and life goals.

The vision was there all along; they just hadn't been able to look up for a long time.

In chapter four, I'll talk about how to organize your time off if you fall into the 89% of people experiencing burnout. If this mini-retirement will be your first, recovering from burnout might be one of your three goals.

CHAPTER ONE

6. Improve health

In 2022, I took a year off; one of my big goals was my health. The pandemic knocked me off course. It was especially hard on my mental health. But it also affected my fitness, nutrition, and stress management. Instead of being thoughtful and intentional in my choices, all things health-related felt disorganized and reactive. I had made small attempts to get things back on track, with little success.

This was my year to prioritize my health.

First up was getting out of my very cloudy area of Montana for the winter. We came up with a plan to be snowbirds, escaping the cold cloudy season for a warmer and sunnier location. Then, I found a group of health and fitness friends to share the journey with. I paid for a health-tracking app. I hired a personal trainer and nutritionist. I read 100+ articles about nutrition and mental health. My psychiatrist recommended I try a low-inflammation lifestyle, which I started experimenting with. By the end of the mini-retirement, I had found new habits and routines that worked for me, and lost 40 pounds.

Many of my coaching clients want to focus on improving their health during their mini-retirements. They want to get eight hours of sleep. They want to reduce their stress and start meditating or doing breathwork. Some want a specific fitness routine, and some just want more movement than they had at a desk job—the small luxuries like taking a walk after breakfast. With more free time and fewer demands, it's easier to cook and feel more thoughtful with nutrition.

Even a month off to prioritize your health and well-being is a game changer. You can experiment with what works for you and design new habits and healthy routines you can maintain when you return to work.

7. Professional growth

I want to share the stories of two coaching clients who used mini-retirements for professional growth.

One, let's call her Rachel, has been in her professional field for a while. She's good at her job. Well compensated. She likes it all right. But she wonders, "Is this what I want to do for the next 20 years?"

Previously, every time a job ended, Rachel rushed to ensure the next one was lined up. During her mini-retirement, she explored what else might be out there. Was there something else that fit her skill set, education, and interests? She took some classes and did a lot of networking. Maybe this would be a significant change, maybe a slight pivot. This time, she spent six months exploring what she wanted to do instead of jumping into the next job.

I have another client we'll call Tom. Tom never felt like the 9–5 corporate world was the best fit for him. He always wondered if he could do something different. Create something on his own. So he saved up to cover six to 12 months of expenses, and he's going to try to scale up his own business. Not only does he want the chance to succeed, he doesn't want the regret of never really trying.

Sometimes career paths seem like the perfect fit, but once you're on one, the reality is quite different. I know many people who went into the medical field because they are kind, compassionate, and empathetic people who wanted to help others, only to have their passion killed by bureaucracy, toxic work environments, and the profit-driven nature of medical care in the U.S.

Sometimes, it's just time for a change. You enjoyed a field for ten or 20 years but can't imagine doing that work for another 20 years. You are ready to try new things, explore new options, and determine what this next act in your work life should look like. Maybe you took the "responsible" career path, but now that you're in a better financial spot you want to circle back to the career you really wanted to do when you were 20 years old.

In our sports half-time analogy, this type of mini-retirement is where you consider switching sports or changing teams. It's ideal to do between jobs and when you have created a longer runway, preferably six months to 18 months. You can use this time to network, take classes, volunteer, and explore possibilities with your skill sets and interests.

8. Test drive retirement

Have you ever met someone who dreamed about doing something for years, even decades, but when they finally tried it, it wasn't what they expected?

I see this a lot in the used fifth-wheel camper market. A couple saves and plans their whole lives so that when they retire they can travel the country together in their camper. It was a great idea on paper, but they never really tested the idea. Three years after hitting the road, the camper is for sale.

Reality rarely matches our imagination. Which is fine unless you have waited and planned and saved for 40 years for that thing. Then it's terribly disappointing. The moral of the story is, don't wait until you are 65 to test, explore, and experiment with what you want your retirement to look like.

While Adam served in the military, we saw our military friends through many life transitions, new babies, deployments, divorces, and retirement. Military members can receive their pension and benefits after 20 years of service, so many retire in their 40s or 50s.

Let me tell you, military retirements rarely go smoothly. When your work takes 40, 50, or 60 hours a week, hobbies, projects, and exploring passions are rare pursuits. Their career is like driving down the highway at 60 miles per hour, and retirement is like throwing the car in reverse. The transition is rocky.

An amazing benefit of mini-retirements is that they allow you to experiment with retirement. It's a bite-size taste, allowing you to practice what retirement might be like. Instead of just a big wish list of things you think you would enjoy, you can go out there and try some of them. Experiment. Cross some things off the list that you don't really like, and add a few new ideas to the list.

Not only will your transition into retirement be smoother if you have had a few practice rounds, but you'll also be more confident about the life you are stepping into. This won't just be a hypothetical, it sounded-like-a-good-idea, type of life. It will be one you have tested and scaled over the years.

9. Long-held dreams

In order to buy our first home, Adam and I saved money for ten years. The house we bought was way under budget because it needed to be gutted and remodeled. With minimal construction experience, we were nervous and overwhelmed by the project. There were no Chip and Joanna Gaines to hold our hands, handle all the work, and reassure us our home would be amazing by the end.

Adam took six months off work and, armed with YouTube videos, we slowly figured it out. Week by week, all the dreams we had about owning a home were happening in front of us. I worked all day and returned home to paint for a few hours before bed. My coworkers thought I was nuts.

About four months after we finished that home, with two months still off work for Adam, we bought our first rental property. If Adam hadn't taken that mini-retirement, there's no way we could have bought and remodeled two homes. While he lost out on six months of income (about $15,000), the rental home has since appreciated $300,000. His taking that time off brought us much closer to financial independence. Mini-retirements don't have to set you back financially; they can slingshot you forward.

Most of us have a dream that we kick around for a while. Sometimes, society talks us out of it. Your friends and family dissuade you with a list of practical reasons. Or schedules and responsibilities kill it. Just because a goal is too hard to fit into life after work, between dinner and bedtime, doesn't make it impossible. If you give yourself a month or a year, you could take on a whole new adventure, hobby, or project.

I have a friend who formed a band in his 50s. He never played in public before, but now they book gigs all summer at birthday parties and local events. He's having a blast. You could use your mini-retirement to get certified as a yoga teacher, write a book, or build a tiny house.

Mini-retirements can breathe new life into old dreams. If you had a year off, what could you give a go? Harper Lee received a year's salary as a gift so she could focus on her writing. That year, she wrote *To Kill a Mockingbird*. Sometimes, those old dreams just need a little nudge. Dust them off.

10. Hard things

I was sitting at a long table with our church's other pastors and staff, having our monthly all-staff meeting. But despite my best efforts to hold the tears down, they kept bubbling up. And pouring out. Finally, I excused myself, and in the tiny church bathroom those tears turned into a flash flood.

I felt stupid and embarrassed. The church secretary came in to check on me. "Honey, are you OK?"

I tried to swallow the sobs and create coherent words but each syllable was punctuated by a sob. I felt like a one-trick pony. My whole life, I coped with trauma by numbing, avoiding, pushing down the pain. But now that trick wasn't working. My feelings wouldn't be pushed down. Instead, they felt like an avalanche barreling down on me, and I feared the avalanche might crush me.

A lot of people have miscarriages. And for a lot of people, it's just a blip. A small setback on their journey to having a baby. At least, that's the way it seemed as an outside observer. But that wasn't my experience.

Grief and pain are like a long, dark tunnel. The only way out is to feel your way through. In the pitch black, you run your hands along the wall and take one small step after another. Depending on how deep the grief is, you might have to grope your way through the tunnel for weeks or months or years. One blind step after another. But I wasn't moving through the grief; I was stuck. Sitting on the floor in the damp, dark tunnel. Attempting to pretend I wasn't in a tunnel of grief. I needed a change.

I needed a mini-retirement: some new experiences, new scenery, and new friends. I asked my employer for a month off. They graciously gave me the month with pay. I think they were relieved. My colleagues had tried their best to comfort me, but their words merely opened up my pain. Everyone was a little overwhelmed and out of their depth.

My best friend was returning from a long stint in Ecuador, and a month-long road trip sounded like the perfect way to ease back into American life. So that's what we did. One month from D.C. to Seattle and back in my Honda Civic. For 6,000 miles, I stared out the window and slowly felt my way through that long, dark tunnel.

Life can be hard in unexpected ways. Loved ones get cancer. People pass away. Homes burn down. Parents need medical care. I get that these hard things aren't associated with a fun and action-packed mini-retirement. Not every mini-retirement needs to be non-stop laughs. And yet, if you give yourself time to focus on working through the hard things, this mini-retirement might prove to be one of your favorites. You can still combine it with one or two other goals, such as spending time with family or improving your health.

One of my coaching clients was very burned out at work as her mom's health declined. This was compounded by the fact her mom lived on another continent. So she took family medical leave for 12 weeks, went overseas, and helped her mom get set up with better medical care assistance. She had time to recover from burnout while having quality time with her mom and helping handle this hard thing.

When faced with a hard and unexpected thing, author Michael Hyatt suggests asking, "What does this make possible?" In every challenge, there are new opportunities that weren't there before. If you have a vision for your mini-retirement, a financial plan ready, and have laid the foundation for your career, you might be able to take a sad song and make it (a little) better.

Which three out of these ten will be the focus of your mini-retirement? These are the main ingredients: the meat, vegetables, and starch of the meal. Now that you know the direction you want to take your mini-retirement, we'll dive into the nuance or spice. The right seasoning makes or breaks a meal. Just a bit more planning, and you'll have the winning recipe.

CHAPTER TWO

THREE TOOLS TO DESIGN A LIFE-CHANGING MINI-RETIREMENT

I was lying on my stomach at the acupuncturist's office. I had never been to an acupuncturist and wasn't sure what to expect. I didn't know if I really believed in acupuncture, but Adam and I had been trying to conceive for a few years, and all the other expensive, stressful, uncomfortable treatments weren't working. Even if the treatment was ineffective, at least lying on the table and chatting with the acupuncturist was relaxing.

He asked what I did for work, and my unenthused response echoed the fact I was deeply unhappy at my current job in sales. But I didn't know what else to do. I had worked as a waitress and at coffee shops, but the crazy hours and standing on my feet all day weren't so appealing anymore. I was OK at sales, mostly because I loved helping and getting to know people. But the competitive nature of it—and backbiting between salespeople—wasn't a good fit. That was the part I dreaded on a Sunday night.

The acupuncturist asked me, "Well, what do you *love* doing?"

I don't know why the question caught me off guard. Perhaps because, for months, I had been looking at it the other way. What was available? What was I qualified for? What kind of experience did I have? Who would hire me? It had been a long time since I asked myself what I *wanted* to do.

Current culture tells us to actively ignore what we want, even what we need. If you asked yourself right now what you want and need, a backlog is likely to pile up. A nap. A fun trip. A weekend at home with no chores. A piece of cake. A night with friends. A glass of water. A walk outside.

That's why you don't ask. You can't take a nap right now. You shouldn't eat the cake. You don't have time for a walk. Your weekend is already full of chores. Instead, we try to silence what we desire. It's depressing to tell ourselves *no* constantly, so we don't allow ourselves to even entertain the question. It's like I say to my kids, before I go into a store with them. "There is no asking for anything."

I thought about his question for a minute as he kept inserting small needles into my back.

What do you love doing?

"I love writing," I said at last.

"Really? That's wonderful. What kind of writing? Novels?" he asked.

"No, I like nonfiction. Essays, I suppose."

"Oh," he seemed disheartened. "I can't imagine there is much of a market for nonfiction essays."

I laughed, "Yeah, not really."

And that should have been the end of it. But the questions kept swirling around my head. What do I love? What do I want? What do I need?

THREE TOOLS

The single biggest mistake I see people make in planning their mini-retirements sounds like this, *"As long as I'm not working, I'll be happy! Anything is better than my current situation."* The difference between a personally life-changing mini-retirement and a mediocre one is about three hours of brainstorming.

In this chapter, I'm going to give you some questions and exercises that will help you unlock the true potential of your mini-retirement. *What do you need? What do you love doing? How can you spend your time in a way that helps you live out your values?* Outside of weekends and short vacations, most people have very little practice at structuring their free time in a way that's meaningful. Don't

CHAPTER TWO

worry too much about what seems feasible or others' expectations. With a few hours' effort you can design your time in a way that gives you exactly what you want—and need.

1. IMAGINE YOUR IDEAL DAY/WEEK/YEAR

A few months after the conversation with the acupuncturist, I found an article online about designing your ideal life. It said to write out an imaginary schedule from morning to night for how you would spend your day. I was in the middle of a grueling year, making it hard to see past the current situation.

But I sat on the edge of my bed, and I wrote out my perfect schedule. There was time for exercise and being outside. There was time to write. Time with the family. And a few hours of focused work each day. I ignored the fact none of this seemed realistic. I tried not to be bogged down with the details of how to navigate from my current life to this fantasy land schedule.

I expanded the exercise to include what an ideal week would look like. Would there be time with friends, religious or spiritual practices, hobbies, or volunteering? Would we do a big weekly outing or activity? Would I see extended family?

Then, I imagined my ideal year. Would there be trips or vacations? Maybe a week of getting the garden set up in the spring? What about holiday celebrations—how much time would I need for those? Maybe I tackle a house project each year or visit friends from college?

Your career break might not look exactly like your ideal day, week, or year. But as you jot things out, it helps you clarify what you need in your life. Look for the elements and themes that appear. How can you bring those specifically into your time off?

For instance, maybe your ideal year blocks out two weeks for

Christmas to have time for fun festive activities, but your sabbatical will be over the summer. You can incorporate the elements of holidays that are meaningful to you—maybe cooking together as a family or gathering with friends. Instead of a holiday, you take those elements that matter to you, add it to another intention like camping, and create a camping vacation complete with friends, family, special meals, and activities.

2. YOUR DREAM TO-DO LIST

To-do lists are an unkind taskmaster, always reminding you there is more to do. They never suggest what you want to do, just the things you should do. For your time off, I want you to create a whole new time-off to-do list. A **dream to-do list**. Not just filled with "shoulds" but with things that will bring you joy, reduce stress, and align with your values.

Especially for driven type-A personalities accustomed to accomplishing a lot of work, adding an hour or two of tasks you can cross off a list can help ease you into your mini-retirement. Too much unstructured and "aimless" time can give ambitious people a feeling of being untethered, bordering on discontent.

For our sixth mini-retirement, Adam and I both took a full year off. We had been in a busy season in life. We bought and remodeled our first house, then bought and remodeled two rentals. We had adopted three siblings and found out we were pregnant. We had a backlog of things to do.

Do you ever feel that way? Like life just keeps piling up faster than you can work through it. Doctor appointments, laundry, repainting the stairs, finding new car insurance, cleaning out the bathroom cupboards. You keep thinking that, at some point, you'll get caught up. Maybe in a few months, things will start to clear out.

But six months later, you somehow have even more things on your to-do list, not fewer.

We started creating our dream to-do list. It was composed of a few categories and, in the end, included over 150 things. It took us almost 18 months to work through it!

Here are some examples:

Regular to-do. This was all the boring stuff. I needed some dental work done and to get life insurance. All that big stuff that's important but not urgent, so week after week it gets pushed off. It doesn't help that they're things you might not really be excited about doing. These things add a white noise of stress to your life because they hang there quietly, nagging you. Clearing a few of these tasks off the list will improve your quality of life when you return to work.

Projects. We had a massive list of projects. During the first month, we tackled a full kitchen remodel for one of our rental houses, repainted our kitchen, and added the master bathroom.

In an attempt to simplify life, I planned to do a full home declutter and reorganization. We had added four kids to our modest home in two years, and our home felt chaotic. Every closet was full, and finding anything was like a scavenger hunt. I knew that going room by room, closet by closet, and drawer by drawer would be a massive undertaking. I committed to touching every item we owned and asking if it truly added value to our home or simply took up space. We spent about four hours a week tackling the decluttering project, which spanned four months. Ultimately, we got rid of about half the things we owned.

Trips. During the four years we lived in Germany, I enjoyed traveling and exploring new places. Moving back to the U.S. was a big adjustment. We had little to no vacation time and had to ask permission to take the kids anywhere before our adoption was finalized. After a few years of staying so close to home, it was exciting to get out and see new places again. We bought a pop-up camper and planned a six-week road trip when the new baby was six months old.

Family and friends. Spending time with family and friends was a big priority for our year off. We had four new family members to introduce to our extended family. We traveled to see our best friends from college. The kids saw grandparents, aunts, uncles and cousins.

Big goals. One of the things on that 150-item list was a very unassuming line, "Something to do with writing." I had no idea that "something" would become a blog, then a coaching and training business, and now, ten years later, this book.

Activities and hobbies. We were the family that loved hiking and camping, except that we weren't doing either before our mini-retirement. Maybe there are activities you loved before, but in the business of life you don't have time for. Or maybe it's things you have wanted to try but never had a real opportunity for. Mini-retirements are perfect for dusting off old hobbies and starting new ones.

Growing up, my small town frequently hosted community dances. As a teenager, I assumed I would learn social dancing as an adult. But it was never in the cards. Until I took a month-long mini-retirement last year to learn tango. I now have a hobby I can enjoy for the rest of my life. And my life is filled with dance, just like I imagined it would be.

We printed off our dream to-do list, and each week we tackled a few things. It gave that first year off some focus, a sense of accomplishment, and structure. As you are planning your time off are there things that would give you a lot of joy or sense of accomplishment to achieve? Looking back on your mini-retirement, what would you be grateful you got done? Are there things that would make your life much easier when you return to work? For many of my coaching clients, having something tangible accomplished during their time off makes them look back on the sabbatical more fondly.

3. IDENTITY. ACTIVITY. POSSESSION.

I read David Bach's *Smart Couples Finish Rich* book shortly after we got married. It had an exercise helping couples think through what they would want to be, have, and do. We have done this thought experiment every year for two decades now.

Before our year off, we went away on a life planning weekend I like to call the **CEO of Your Life Retreat**. In my full geeky mode, I had packed paper, pens, markers, Post-it notes, and posterboard for our romantic weekend. We discussed ideas over coffee dates, dinners, and long walks downtown. Back at the hotel room, I pulled out the poster board and Post-its to do an adapted version of David Bach's be-have-do exercise.

We started with "Identity." What were all the things we wanted to be core to our identity? How would we want others to know us? What kinds of words would we use to introduce ourselves? How would we want others to introduce us?

We sat on the floor and tried to think up five or ten words. Mine were things like a relaxed and happy mom, a writer, reader, traveler, gardener, and entrepreneur (although I had no idea how that might look.)

Then we moved on to "Activity." What kinds of activities mattered to us? Some of those correlated to our identity, like travel and reading. Adam added car repair. I jotted down renovating properties, local adventures with the kids, reading, volunteering, date nights with Adam, and learning new skills.

The last set of Post-it notes was for "Possessions"—what things did we want to own? What possessions felt necessary or essential to help facilitate our identity and activities? Library card, a camper, a lovely yard and garden, made my list.

Adam and I each discussed what the words meant to us and why they were important. We talked about all the Post-it notes that matched each other's and the ones that were very different. Classic cars and downhill skiing made the top of his list and were nowhere to be found on mine.

Thousands of people have done these exercises either from my video courses, at events, or during coaching. I think it's one of the simplest ways to start imagining what your mini-retirement could look like. People rarely write down 1,000 things. Often, there are only five, ten, or 20 items in each category. The things that make it on the Post-it notes are the ones that matter the most. It cuts through the noise, marketing, and others' expectations of you. Who do you want to be? What do you want to do? What possessions make those first two easier?

As you look at these Post-it notes that are so closely tied to your identity and your values, think about how you could layer these into your day or other big activities you have planned. If one of your big three goals is travel, and you wrote down reading for an activity, maybe you could load your e-reader with books and take time to read each day while you travel. If an activity goal was spending time outside, you could do your reading in a park while you travel. If an activity was baking, maybe you do your reading in different bakeries while you travel. The idea is to layer these "identity, activities and possessions" into your big three goals. **Value layering** is about finding one activity that combines a few different values. For example, if one of your big three goals is getting healthier, and you also wrote down time outside and time with friends, you could meet up with a friend to go for a walk outside.

CHAPTER TWO

> Value layering isn't about overfilling your schedule. Instead, find one thing that fulfills a few intentions or values. The more you layer these values, the richer your time off will become.

CRAFTING YOUR PLAN

Of the three tools, one might have made perfect sense to you and really resonated. Another one was a flop. That's perfectly normal and why there are three tools to pick from instead of a one-size-fits-all approach.

Hopefully, you have pages of ideas. Sticky notes are all over the place. I hope you are buzzing with the possibilities. You might have enough inspiration to fill a dozen mini-retirements.

If you find your bucket list is still a little lean, here are a few extra questions to consider.

1. Does anything feel urgent for this first mini-retirement?
2. What is important to focus on right now?
3. As the seasons of life are speeding up, what do you feel your window of opportunity closing on?

When you look back on this decade of your life, what do you want to define it? If you could give it a theme, what would it be? When I look back on my 20s, it was a season of international travel and personal growth. My 30s were full of professional exploration and making incredible memories with my kids. When I get to 50 and reflect on my 40s, how do I want to describe these years?

Which of these goals or intentions fit into the amount of time off work available to you? Maybe you would love a year-long around-the-world trip but, at the moment, you can only get a month off. Brainstorm things you can accomplish in a month, and save the big trip for later.

Visualize yourself at 80 years old, sitting on the porch, full of a lifetime of wisdom and experience. Ask your older self what they wish you would have done on this mini-retirement. Knowing what they know now, what advice would they share with you? What would they encourage you towards? And if you did that thing, do they regret it? Taking five minutes for this exercise can give tremendous clarity about the things hidden in us but never fully articulated.

… CHAPTER THREE

CHOOSING YOUR NEXT ADVENTURE

Waiting in the medspa office, I started chatting with the receptionist. Bubbling with excitement, she told everyone who would listen about the adventure she had just returned from. This trip was her first time on an airplane, the first time she had even left the state of Montana. Now curious and invested in the story, I asked, "Where did you go?"

"Peru," she said. "And not just the cities, I went into the jungles. I spent a whole month there. I've never had an experience like that in my life!"

Now I was dumbfounded. I had to make sure I had these details right, "So, for your very first airplane trip, you went to the deepest, darkest jungles of Peru like you were searching for Paddington Bear?" Thirty days and a few thousand dollars later, she had returned from the adventure of a lifetime.

Sometimes, people push back when I mention mini-retirements because they think they are only available to high earners. But I took many mini-retirements when I was earning $25,000. There is a mini-retirement for every budget. And a mini-retirement for every profession. No matter if you're a receptionist, electrician, or lawyer.

Hopefully, you finished the last two chapters with a pile of ideas of things you could do. Now I want to look at which mini-retirement you should take next. If you have 20 amazing adventures to choose from, how do you decide on the order you take them in? My goal isn't just to give you one incredible career break but a lifetime of adventures. There are a few different tools you can use to sort out which one to take next, and think through how you'd map them out throughout your life.

Maybe you start with an epic, but affordable, journey to Peruvian jungles. Or if your jungle hiking days are past you, a more pricey European river cruise is the next mini-retirement.

SEQUENCE OF EVENTS

Let's say you have 20 amazing adventures you'd love to take. Maybe learning to play guitar, earning a blackbelt, a massive national park road trip, learning French, biking through Europe, and an around-the-world cruise. Where do you start? If you are early in your wealth-building journey, one way to narrow down which thing to do first is to start with the lower-cost options.

The order in which you take these mini-retirements will have a massive impact on your financial progress. As a thought experiment, let's say you have 20 of these adventures on your bucket list. For the sake of simplicity, they happen to cost $1,000, $2,000, $3,000, all the way to the 20th adventure costing $20,000.

You plan to do all 20, no changes, no exceptions. But what if you are thoughtful about the *order* in which they happen? Instead of starting with the $20,000 adventure, like the around-the-world cruise, you start with the $1,000 mini-retirement, which could be learning to play the guitar. And each year thereafter, you do the one which costs $1,000 more. That's Plan A.

Plan B: you start with the $20,000 adventure and take the mini-retirements in descending cost.

Now, let's assume you have $20,000 a year to split between your mini-retirement and investing. Here's how each plan looks:

CHAPTER THREE

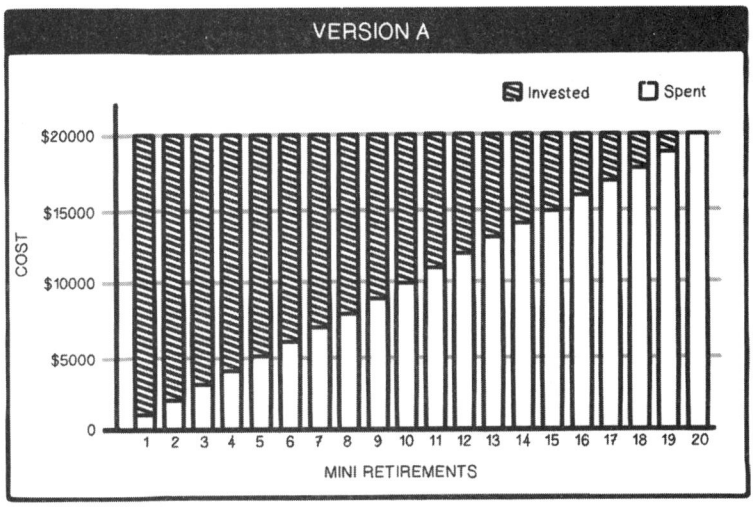

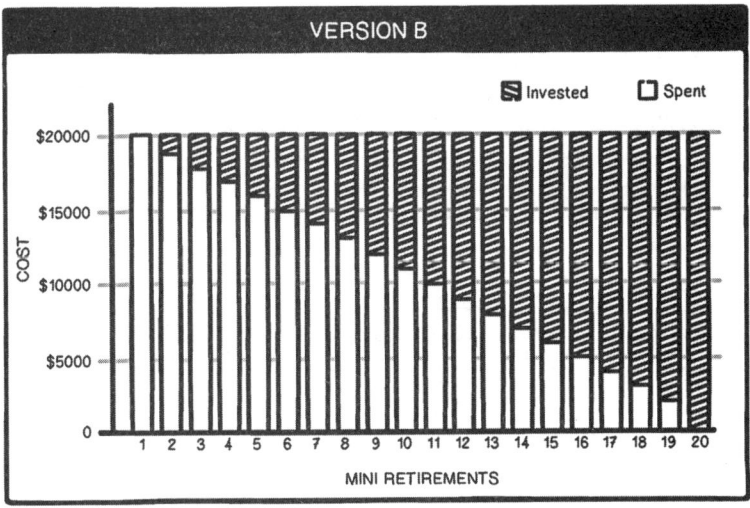

You will spend the exact same amount of money in Plan A and Plan B, totaling $210,000. And you'll invest the exact same amount of money, $190,000. **The only difference between Plan A and B is the sequence of events.**

If you take the more expensive mini-retirements first, you end up with $299,935 invested. Start with the affordable options, and you have $478,978. *That's an extra $179,043.* $179,000 is a big bonus for just being thoughtful about the sequence of events. Of course, you don't have to start with the more affordable options. But if you are trying to narrow down ten amazing ideas, it's worth considering starting with more affordable options.

Year	Version A		Version B	
	Invested	Total Investment	Invested	Total Investment
1	19000	$19,000.00	0	$0.00
2	18000	$38,330.00	1000	$1,000.00
3	17000	$58,013.10	2000	$3,070.00
4	16000	$78,074.02	3000	$6,284.90
5	15000	$98,539.20	4000	$10,724.84
6	14000	$119,436.94	5000	$16,475.58
7	13000	$140,797.53	6000	$23,628.87
8	12000	$162,653.35	7000	$32,282.89
9	11000	$185,039.09	8000	$42,542.70
10	10000	$207,991.83	9000	$54,520.69
11	9000	$231,551.25	10000	$68,337.13
12	8000	$255,759.84	11000	$84,120.73
13	7000	$280,663.03	12000	$102,009.18
14	6000	$306,309.44	13000	$122,149.83
15	5000	$332,751.10	14000	$144,700.31
16	4000	$360,043.68	15000	$169,829.34
17	3000	$388,246.74	16000	$197,717.39
18	2000	$417,424.01	17000	$228,557.61
19	1000	$447,643.69	18000	$262,556.64
20	0	$478,978.75	19000	$299,935.60

So the first filter for which mini-retirement to take next is looking at all the options, affordable to expensive. Don't worry if you don't know the exact cost for these mini-retirements, that's what Step Three later in the book will help you with.

CHAPTER THREE

THE FOUR QUADRANTS OF COST AND HEALTH

I'm the perfect age. Every year, in fact. On my birthday, I sit down and list out all the reasons why the age I'm turning is the perfect age. Every age is the perfect age for something. Forty-one is the perfect age for me to work on my strength training. Sixty-three will be the perfect age for me to take long trips with my girlfriends. Seventy-six will be the perfect age to meet up for coffee daily with the local crowd.

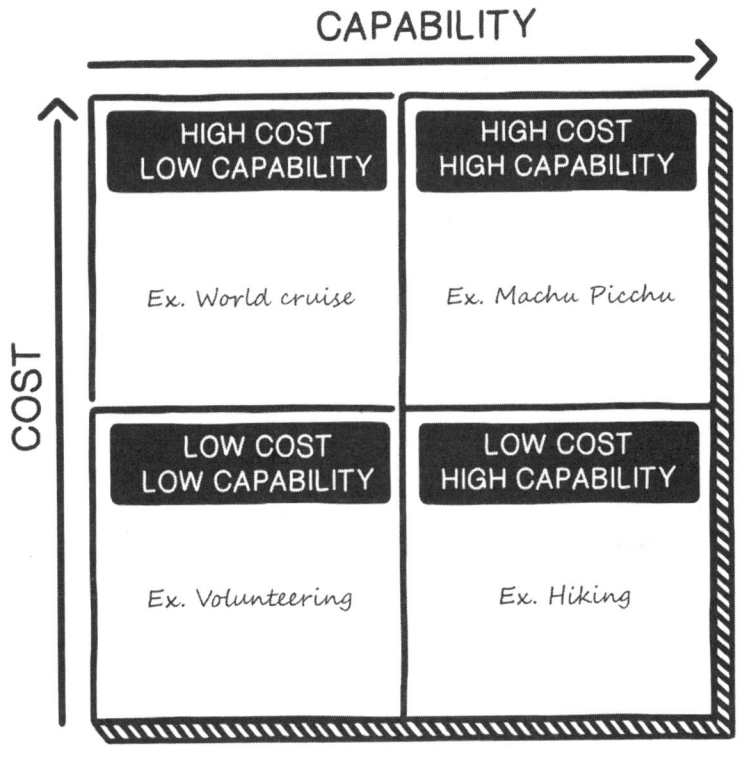

Our health and fitness aren't static. You might have some limitations you are already dealing with. In my 20s, I had dreamed of hiking Machu Picchu, but after an injury my back tightens up every time I carry a backpack or walk too long. Unfortunately, I've had to cross that dream off, unfulfilled. Looking over your list of adventures and dreams, are there things that you will need more health and fitness to accomplish and enjoy?

You can map out your ideas on a cost and capability quadrant. I like to think about what each decade in life might look like. No one knows the future, but you might have a sense of how much capability you can expect. Seeing all the adventures I have planned into my 60s and 70s also motivates me to focus on my strength training in my 40s.

For example, if you are in your 20s and 30s, you might prioritize the low-cost/high-capability activities. Road trips, hiking, camping, volunteering, and learning new skills or cultivating hobbies you'll enjoy for decades to come. You could save some of the high-cost/low-capability activities for your 60s or 70s. Fancy hotels in Paris, guided tours, and cruises are very enjoyable in your senior years.

THE TIME-LUXURY FACTOR

A common mistake people make when planning a mini-retirement is extrapolating the cost based on their vacation experiences. Not factoring in what I call the **time-luxury factor**.

When your time is very limited, you need to squeeze in as much enjoyment as possible. This is true for a week-long trip to Paris or a date night after a busy week at work. If you only have three hours for your date, you might opt to hire a sitter ($75), go to a restaurant ($60), and take in a movie ($30). Your three hours end up costing $165. Imagine if, instead, after a relaxing week at home, you had all day Saturday to spend with the family. You might grab a coffee ($10),

CHAPTER THREE

get the kids some kettle corn at the farmers' market ($10), hang out at a park, and grab some food at the grocery deli for a picnic ($30). The whole day costs $50 versus your $165 three-hour date.

The time-luxury factor shows that the more time you have, the less luxury you need. The less time you have, the more luxury you might want.

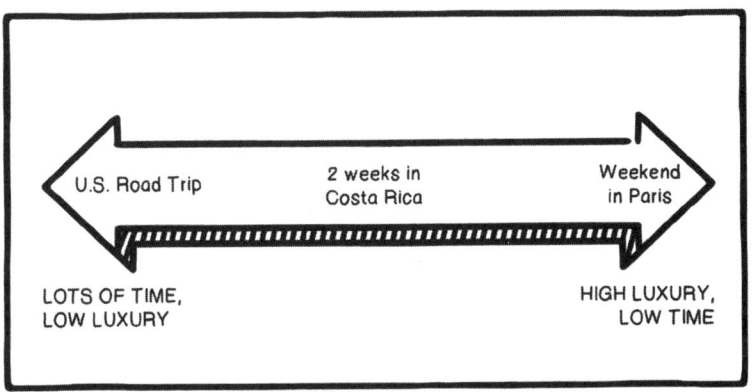

Slow travel, casual long weekends, and time-intensive hobbies can be much more affordable. The week-long trip to Paris might cost $3,000. I know many families who live in France for $3,000 a month. Not that you shouldn't see Paris, but if you have three months in France, you might spend one week there, then the rest of the time in more affordable places.

When Adam and I traveled around the U.S. in our camper, we easily spent less than $3,000 a month. In fact, we usually rented our home out while we were gone, and that income alone covered most of our travel costs.

If you are traveling for three months, it should look different than a week-long trip. Most people don't enjoy eating out 270 meals in a row. So you might do some grocery shopping for an easy breakfast or lunch. You don't need to see four sights daily, 90 days straight. You can spend a whole afternoon at a café or city square. You can take naps, read books, or sign up for classes. You'll still see all the sights but at a slower pace. Give yourself enough time, and the simple pleasures of life will naturally make your trip more affordable.

PHASES OF THE CAREER BREAK

Hopefully, these tools give you a way to sort through your bucket list and pick the next mini-retirement. As you start planning out the specifics of this career break, remember how you picked out three focuses? Depending on the length, you can break it up into phases. Not everything needs to happen at the same time.

In each phase, which might last from weeks to months, you have a main focus. Let's say your three goals were rest, family time, and a creative project, and you have three months off. You could spend the first three weeks just resting. Then it's a holiday, and you focus on family activities for five weeks. You finish your time with four weeks where creative projects become the priority.

This mental framework helps accomplish two things.

1. **Permission.** Should you take that nap? Is it OK if you spend the whole afternoon hiking? What about that creative project you said you wanted to do? Knowing that you are in your rest phase, you have permission to rest. That's the goal you set; allow yourself to prioritize it. You are doing exactly what you said you were going to do. Labeling the phase and setting that intention gives you permission.
2. **Confidence.** But what about all those other things you said you were going to do? It doesn't have to happen today. It's on the calendar. Those things have their time and place. You can feel confident that you will get to those things. You haven't forgotten

them. Settle into your phase knowing that the other goals will also get done in due time.

Have you ever had a boss give you ten different tasks and say all were top priority? It's hard to know if you are working on the right thing at the right time. It's stressful. But if your boss says, work on this one thing, those other things we will start next month—you can settle into the task at hand. Be a good boss to yourself. Allow yourself to focus on one goal at a time. Set the priority, knowing there is a specific time for everything.

CHAPTER FOUR

RECOVER FROM BURNOUT

WHEN I WAS a teenager, I thought middle age naturally makes people boring. Something about growing up made people lose their creativity, spontaneous joy, and zest for life. Adults seemed tired and stressed, always opting for the easiest and smallest options. They didn't dream big dreams or chase adventurous goals.

Now that I'm middle-aged and raising kids, I realize life fills up with bills and chores. But also, we are simply tired. Too tired to muster the gumption for big adventures and chasing wild dreams. Research bears this out as well. Depending on the survey, about 50% to 89% of Americans are experiencing some form of burnout and chronic exhaustion.

Maybe we didn't become boring, just burned out?

Burnout is a bit like fasting. Our bodies are incredibly adaptable. They can withstand periods of stress and go without food for days. Both of which are incredibly useful skills. For most of human history, we haven't had 24/7 access to food. And life could be stressful: war, sickness, death, drought. So we needed to adapt to survive these brief challenges. In most parts of the world, we eliminated the stress of going without food but went in the opposite direction with stress. We traded occasional stress for constant stress.

Fasting and stress are similar in that they both affect you mentally, emotionally, chemically, and physically. And they both serve the same goal: to get you out of the situation! You are able to fast in order to find food. You can withstand stress in order to get to a place for you to find rest.

In times of fasting, your body adapts so that you have the energy to find more food. Your body is even clever enough to reduce your hunger pains, so that you aren't too distracted in your search for food. But the goal of this isn't you never eating again. The goal is to find food. And if you don't find food, starvation sets in.

It's the same with stress. The function of stress is to help you get out of a stressful situation. In order to keep you focused, unessential things start to drop off. You lose creativity, joy, and enthusiasm. All of these are distractions. Big dreams and ambitious goals have no place when you need to focus on survival.

Imagine you are on a nature hike. Birds singing, a bubbling creek, wildflowers blowing in the breeze. But if you are in danger, your mind and eyes focus. *"Don't look around and take it all in; stay focused. Get out. Keep your eyes on the path. Keep moving."* All of this is useful. Yet you miss the wonders around you. This is the early stage of burnout. Stress and burnout have one function: to enable you to get out of the situation. The message is, *"Keep going! Get out! Get out! Get out! Keep going in order to get out!"* Burnout is *not* your body helping you thrive in stressful situations. You are not thriving. Your body is trying to help you survive long enough to get you out of there.

Just like fasting, during burnout you don't feel the full weight of your fatigue. Many people are shocked at how intensely tired they feel when a few weeks into their mini-retirement their cortisol starts to drop, and they begin to relax. It's like starting to eat after fasting. As soon as your body realizes that food is available, those hunger signals come rushing back, and people stay hungry until their body is replenished. When your body senses it has full access to rest, you'll experience the full effect of your burnout. And you will stay tired until you are fully recovered. We will cover how to navigate this more in Step Four, because the "downshift" feeling can be intense and unexpected.

Just like there is a tipping point between fasting and starvation, the same is true for burnout. Your body can adapt for so long, but then more serious and long-term consequences happen. Burnout

CHAPTER FOUR

will cause both structural and functional dysregulation of central neural pathways, a decrease in brain matter, decreased cognitive function, physical fatigue, and possibly psychological disorders. Remember you are not built to thrive in constant stress; you are surviving long enough to get out of the stressful situation.

ACTIVE REST

So, how do we recover from burnout? Contrary to what some people might think, it isn't done by lounging around in our pajamas and watching TV all day. You need to be thoughtful and intentional about this transition, especially if coming from a high-stress and highly productive career. I like to design a schedule filled with **active rest**. If your life and work have been demanding and highly scheduled, the transition is often easier if you *schedule* restful activities into your time off.

Active rest activities are anything that's restful for you and you could write on a to-do list. This looks like a morning walk or an exercise class for some people. It could be meditation or reading a book. Maybe you enjoy going for a hike, going out to lunch with a friend, hosting a game night, or a dinner party. I encourage clients to find **four to six active rest activities** to do each day during their recovery.

There are three methods to organize your daily active rest. Experiment with all three to see which works best.

1. To-do list
2. Schedule
3. Inspiration.

With the to-do list, you'll write out which active rest tasks you want to incorporate that day or week. Check them off as you go.

That way, at the end of the day, you'll know you've done exactly what you needed to do.

To do
- ☐ Read for 30 minutes
- ☐ Meditate with an app for 15 minutes
- ☐ Walk the dog in the morning
- ☐ Sit outside and drink coffee
- ☐ Call a friend
- ☐ Organize the downstairs closet
- ☐ Get drinks with friends at 7 p.m.

You could also create a loose schedule that builds in active rest with a system of loose time blocks:

Morning
- ☐ 6–7 Coffee, breakfast, read
- ☐ 7–9 Kids to school
- ☐ 9–11 Go for a walk, meditate, journal
- ☐ 11–12 Lunch with a friend

Afternoon
- ☐ 12–3 Garden
- ☐ 3–5 Kids and dinner prep
- ☐ 7–8 TV
- ☐ 8–10 Read, bedtime

CHAPTER FOUR

Your third option is the inspiration list. Spring/summer 2024 was one of the hardest six months of my life. Not burnout, but personal crisis after personal crisis felt like small explosions, leaving me in a state of shock and grief.

A to-do list would have felt like a burden, a time-block schedule seemed unrealistic. So I created three categories and filled each with activities that were helpful in that season.

Anytime I felt stuck or confused as to what I should do next, I simply looked at the inspiration sheet and picked one that felt right. My inspo sheet looked a little like this:

***

Health
- ❏ Journal
- ❏ Therapy
- ❏ Walking
- ❏ Food prep
- ❏ Hot tea
- ❏ Gardening
- ❏ Reading
- ❏ Massage
- ❏ Hot bath
- ❏ Dry herbs

Connection
- ❏ Phone call
- ❏ Time with Mom
- ❏ Texting
- ❏ Coffee with friends
- ❏ Time with family

Work
- ❏ Coaching/teaching
- ❏ Record podcast
- ❏ Write
- ❏ Planning meeting with assistant

UN-RUSHING

Rushing is how we survive busy and stressful seasons of life. Rush through breakfast, rush to work, rush through meetings, rush home, rush to pick up kids, rush to make dinner. Always rushing. It keeps us in a high-cortisol, high heart rate, elevated state. Keep moving, because if you slow down, you might feel too tired to start rushing again.

If you want to recover from burnout, you need to practice un-rushing. Take the normal tasks of life and slow them down. Cook slowly. Eat slowly. Drink coffee slowly. Breath slowly. Vacuum slowly.

Rushing is a learned pattern, and even when it's no longer necessary it can be a tough pattern to break. Practice as much as you can before you start your mini-retirement, which will give you a head start on this skill. Pick one type of activity to do in a slow and relaxed way. If you are pulled back into that rushing energy, take a slow five-second breath and try un-rushing again.

Whenever I feel extra stuck in an old pattern and need a little woo to get me unstuck, I will thank the old pattern and let it know its service is not needed right now. In this case it would sound like, *"I appreciate how much this rushing has helped me be productive and survive in the past, but right now it isn't required. This is an un-rushing situation. I'm intentionally doing this in a relaxed way. I'll be sure to let you know when I need your help again."*

> Recovering from burnout always takes longer than people anticipate. Even a mild case of burnout can take a month. For more severe cases, six months to a year is really common. When people are given the chance and opportunity to take longer breaks, I see their spark of creativity and motivation start to grow back at two or three years, even if they assumed they would retire forever.

CHAPTER FOUR

> While recovering from burnout in the place that created burnout is not impossible, it is very challenging. Often, what's needed is time and space away from the thing that created the stress and the fatigue. It would be like trying to reduce your stress while a bear is still chasing you. In order to calm your nervous system, you need to know the bear is nowhere nearby. Once you're in a safe and healthy spot, your nervous system can relax, your cortisol levels can go down, and you can start to recover.
>
> I often have coaching clients who want a major professional change. The trouble is they can't even imagine what that could look like. A mini-retirement creates the perfect opportunity to recover from this burnout. Slowly, as the days and weeks pass, your creativity returns. You see more possibilities.

Burnout is so prevalent in our culture that most people accept it as the norm. Meeting someone who feels creative, fresh, intuitive, and full of life sets them apart. I always encourage clients to try to recover as much as possible from burnout before starting a new job. In an interview, it's incredibly difficult to hide our body language and micro-expressions. Because burnout is so prevalent, it's easy to recognize. Especially when you're in the interview talking about starting a new career, it's hard to hide the sense of being overwhelmed and dreading the prospect of something new and challenging. Returning to the workforce refreshed, excited, and full of life greatly improves your chances of finding the perfect next job.

Now, let's dive into Step Two, which is all about employment: negotiating a break from work, crafting your sabbatical story, and finding your incredible job after a career break.

STEP TWO

UNEXPECTED CAREER BENEFITS

CHAPTER FIVE

UPLEVEL YOUR CAREER

WHILE MY FAMILY and I were traveling, I met up with Kevin, who had taken a year-long mini-retirement. This time away had clearly been a boost to his happiness as he began by focusing on health, rest, and hobbies. By the middle of his year off, he really wanted to explore what other career options might be interesting for him. He became interested in a new industry and started taking classes to gain the necessary skills. By the end of his mini-retirement, he had enough skills to be offered a job in this new profession.

People always ask me, *"How in the world does giving up a year of pay and spending a bunch of money help a person financially, let alone professionally?"* Kevin's experience echoes what I've seen time and again. Your best opportunity for getting a significant pay bump is by switching companies, and—perhaps counterintuitively—mini-retirements are one of the best ways of unlocking this opportunity. Kevin returned to a new job at 150% of his previous salary. This will have a massive impact on his lifetime earning potential, not only enabling him to retire earlier but also afford more mini-retirements until then. He also received a sign-on bonus at his new job, which covered 60% of the cost of his year off.

I was delighted hearing about the success of his mini-retirement, but not surprised. Taking a sabbatical offers a multitude of professional benefits. Here are the three that I see most often.

RETIRE OFTEN

1. BETTER JOB OFFERS

The best way to get a 20%+ raise is by switching jobs. While I've helped clients get up to a 50% raise at a current employer, it takes a good deal of skill and luck. Your best bet is to find a company that values all the professional growth you've acquired since you were last hired.

Taking a mini-retirement offers a few tactical benefits vs just switching jobs. Switching jobs can feel like a hassle, but a mini-retirement provides the perfect motivation to make a change. A mini-retirement can also help you recover from burnout or build new professional skills. As you will learn in this section, you leverage your time away to elicit better job offers.

Part of the reason Kevin was able to find a job at 150% of his old salary was that he had been with the same employer for a long time. He had left a lot of money on the table by not taking sabbaticals more frequently.

2. UPGRADE YOUR JOB

In this part of the book, I will show you how to negotiate a sabbatical from your current employer. But we will also discuss negotiating a better job *with* your current employer. It's a creative and collaborative process when people begin these sabbatical conversations. While the conversations are happening, asking for other accommodations is fairly easy. Maybe you redesign your job role, and add more work-from-home days or adjust your hours. It's like remodeling your kitchen, there is a *"while we are at it, we might as well…"* attitude. All of this can be advantageous. You get a sabbatical and can find ways to improve your job when you return.

On my podcast, Diania shared her experience negotiating her sabbatical which allowed her to hike the Camino trail. When she returned, she then negotiated 100% work from home that allowed her to move from the very expensive New York City to Ohio. She was able to buy a home and met a midwest gentleman whom she married. The mini-retirement was like a series of dominos creating professional, financial, and personal growth.

3. CAREER PIVOT

Many of us have a moment at some point in our careers when we ask, *"Am I really going to do this until I'm 65?"* Like Kevin, you can use your mini-retirement to explore new career options by taking classes and building new skills.

In my group coaching, many people explore new career options, especially if they have made good progress on their financial goals. I call it the **Second Chapter Career**. A First Chapter Career is about earning the most possible, paying off debt, and building a foundation of financial security. A Second Chapter Career isn't just optimizing for the most money. In a Second Chapter Career, people often want more purpose. They want work that aligns with their skill set and passions. They want time and space for the things they value: health, family, hobbies. They want to work with interesting people and do interesting things. Even if it pays less.

Money isn't the only goal in a Second Chapter Career. Some people never get a Second Chapter Career. But with the financial progress and clarity you will gain from taking mini-retirements, you will have an opportunity for a Second Chapter Career if you desire one.

Figuring out what your Second Chapter Career could be takes time—time for reflection, exploration, conversation, and curiosity. That kind of process doesn't pair well alongside a 60-hour-a-week, stressful job.

THREE NEGOTIATIONS

In this step, you'll learn the three types of negotiation: taking a sabbatical, exit negotiation, and adjusting your current job. We will go over how to network for your next job. Plus, how self-employed and business owners can prepare their businesses for their sabbatical. But all of this starts with your mini-retirement story. How you craft the narrative is essential in order to leverage your mini-retirement into professional growth.

CHAPTER SIX

CRAFTING YOUR MINI-RETIREMENT STORY

A GOOD STORY WILL pull you in. Captivate your attention. Spark your imagination. And stick with you. You'll need to tell your mini-retirement story numerous times: while negotiating time off, explaining to your coworkers, telling friends and family, or during interviews for future jobs. Crafting a compelling story that rallies others to support you is worth the time and effort. Plus you'll want a story you feel confident and comfortable telling. If you fumble the story, you will invite confusion, questions, and concerns into the conversation.

We learn to tell stories by hearing stories told. Stories of friendship, adventure, or how people met and fell in love. The first challenge with learning to tell your career break story is that you might not have heard many of them. In this chapter, I'm going to give you a lot of examples of how people describe their career-break plans.

The second challenge to crafting a career-break story is the cultural or familial baggage you might bring to the story. For many, "hard work" means continuous work. Hard work means sacrifice and suffering. It means being "realistic" and letting go of childish dreams or goals. If you are having too much fun, relaxing too much, or pursuing hobbies, it's a sign that you aren't serious or perhaps even lack moral strength.

People sometimes struggle to escape these narratives. They struggle even more to believe that others will see past them when hearing about their mini-retirement. *"What if they think I'm not hardworking, dedicated or capable at my work?"* First, let's fact-check this. Are you hardworking, dedicated, and capable? The answer usually is yes. Now, your task becomes sharing the story that highlights that truth.

MEMOIR RULES

The two rules of writing a memoir are: 1. Everything must be true. 2. It can't be the whole truth.

When crafting the story explaining your career break, everything you say must be true. This isn't the place to lie or create some fantasy. But, just like a memoir, it can't be the whole truth. The whole truth is simply too vast to explain it all. You could write a 'roo thousand word book, and it wouldn't be the whole truth. **If you try to tell the whole truth, you'll lose the story.** Have you ever met that person who tries to tell you every detail of a story and, 30 minutes in, you have no idea what they are even talking about? You just pray it ends soon. This can't be the fate of your mini-retirement story.

Because you can't tell the whole story, you need to figure out which parts of the story you will tell. Ideally, your story will contain five elements: positive, interesting, specific, time-sensitive, and one-time events. Try to include as many as appropriate to craft your story.

> It may feel like we're leaping ahead here. You haven't even started the conversation with your employer! But it's important to set the foundation for your mini-retirement by establishing how you will describe it. All of this will of course naturally feed into how you then pitch it to your boss or discuss it in interviews.

CHAPTER SIX

POSITIVE

The story you pick should be positive. Portray it in an uplifting light. Even if your sabbatical contained difficult circumstances, find a positive outcome in the story and finish with that.

For example, the negative (and true) version might sound like, *"My last job was awful. I stuck it out for years, but it took a toll on me. I was so burned out by the time I left, I just needed some time to get my head back on straight. There was no way I could have jumped into another job right away."*

The positive (and also true) version might sound like, *"I've always been interested in yoga and meditation. I never really had time to focus on it. When the opportunity for a small career break came up, I knew that's what I wanted to do a deep dive into. I started a daily practice and then spent a month at a retreat center in Thailand studying with some great practitioners. It was a once-in-a-lifetime experience. Now, I feel like I can maintain this daily practice for the rest of my life. Having this new habit has been incredibly transformative."*

Both stories are true, but one highlights the positive outcome.

Another example of the two sides of a story. The negative version might sound like, *"My mom was diagnosed with Alzheimer's, and it was devastating. I couldn't focus on work and felt so distracted and guilty. My work and my mom's care felt subpar. So I had to quit. Getting her settled into a nursing home was really hard. I was responsible for figuring out the bills and selling her house. It was a hard transition, but she is doing better now. It's definitely time to get back to work."*

A more positive way to tell this story could be, *"When my mom was diagnosed with Alzheimer's, it was a hard transition for her. Thankfully, I was able to step away from my job for six months. I'm so grateful that I had that time to support her. Moving into a nursing home wasn't easy, but being able to give her all my time and attention took away a lot of the stress. I was able to sort out all the bills, get her house sold, and make sure everything was set up for her future. She* had a lot of good days during that time, and those are memories I'll cherish forever."

When you're talking to your current or future boss, you have to remember they are also human. They share many of the same dreams, goals, struggles, and desires as you. Pursuing those things during a mini-retirement might be unusual, but the goal or desire isn't. We want time with people we love, adventure, personal growth, to rest, play, learn something new, and engage with our interests. These are all common to our humanity.

INTERESTING

Another factor is choosing an interesting angle for your story. Even when it comes to planning your mini-retirement, pick at least one interesting thing to do during your time away. It doesn't have to be the bulk of your time, just something others will find interesting. These will also be the things you will probably remember fondly long after your sabbatical.

An uninteresting story might be, *"I really wanted to spend more time with my family. My last job was really demanding, and I missed out on a lot of their childhood. The six months I took off helped me catch up on those life events."*

Highlighting one element of the story can make this more interesting. *"I've always wanted to take my kids to national parks. I had such amazing memories of doing that as a child; all of us loaded in the back of the car. For my mini-retirement, we did a road trip, hitting ten different parks. We saw the Grand Canyon, Arches, Yellowstone and drove up the Going-to-the-Sun Road in Glacier. It was an incredible few weeks. I've always been very committed in my work positions, and sometimes that has meant not doing big trips with the kids. This time away helped us cross a major item off our bucket list. It was an incredible experience."*

CHAPTER SIX

SPECIFIC EVENTS

If possible, spend some time doing a specific event during your mini-retirement. People can cheer on a specific event and get more excited about that. It not only helps give you a stronger story but also makes your time more memorable. If your goal is to learn to cook a new cuisine, you could take a cooking class. If you want to improve your mental health, you could try a silent meditation event. Maybe you want to hike more; instead of just saying you hiked more, is there a specific hike you could highlight? As you look through the planning you did in Step One, is there a specific event that could highlight the purpose of your time off?

ONE-TIME EVENTS

A one-time event helps suggest that you won't be constantly asking for large chunks of time off. I love to garden, but if I complete the Master Gardener certification it's a one-time event, not something that happens repeatedly. Classes or certifications are good for this. It can also be a specific event that people rarely do more than once, like a significant hike or volunteering overseas.

For example, in explaining a career gap on your resume, *"During that year, I was able to volunteer teaching children English in Vietnam for six months. It was an incredible experience with the kids and a great education for me in understanding how non-profits work. I gained a lot of insight into how to communicate an organization's culture and mission in a way that inspires people to give above and beyond. The kids learned a lot, but unexpectedly it was also a time of incredible professional growth for me."*

TIME-SENSITIVE EVENTS

The activity itself could be time-sensitive. It gives clarity on why this event needed to happen now vs later. Birthdays, anniversaries, and big life events can create a time-sensitive life goal. Hiking in Ireland for your dad's 60th birthday. Building homes with Habitat for Humanity for your honeymoon. Writing a book before you turn 40. Spending a month in Paris for your 25th wedding anniversary.

Uninspiring story: *"My last job was so busy I never could focus on my health. I really wanted to get in shape. Taking some time off helped me focus on that."*

Inspiring story (positive, interesting, specific, one-time, and time-sensitive): *"I don't know why, but I always dreamed of participating in a triathlon before I turned 50. When I hit 49, I knew it was now or never. They host a triathlon in Hawaii each year, which was the perfect way to celebrate turning 50. My work has always been a priority, so I was kind of starting from scratch on my fitness. I took three months and hired a personal trainer. It was an intense experience but really incredible. I wasn't the fastest one out there, but I did pretty well for 50. Physically and mentally, I feel better than I did at 30."*

When you are picking your next mini-retirement, think about if there is one anchor event that can help tell the story. For example, every ten years in Germany, a small village hosts the Passion play. It's an incredible event that has taken place since 1633. After living in Germany for four years and taking five semesters of German language, I was able to see the play in 2010 and still only understand 10% of what was said. That would be a positive, interesting, specific, one-time, time-sensitive event to highlight.

Your mini-retirement will contain many themes. But your job isn't to tell every story. Instead, pick one thing and tell that story well. Having a story that contains these elements will draw people into your story and maybe leave them feeling inspired or a bit jealous.

CHAPTER SIX

INDUSTRY-SPECIFIC CONCERNS

Some industries have their own specific concerns. As with many negotiating aspects, you want to voice the concern someone might be thinking with your version of the story *before* they do. Think through what their concerns might be, and have your perspective ready.

For example, some industry cultures are hyper-competitive and look down on the idea of work-life balance. Any personal life you maintain is a sign of weakness. If that's the kind of company and culture you want to return to, then lean into that story. Make it a work hard, play hard story. One where you give 100% of your life to your work, then in between jobs you go extreme on adventure, recreation, or other goals, so that you can come back and hyper-focus on your work.

If the concern is credentials, licensing, or education, be ready to talk about how you planned for those things. People from all kinds of professions have taken time away from work. For some, it was medical leave, family emergencies, or having children. Others having taken planned mini-retirements. Whatever the obstacle, there is a solution. **Your job is to understand the cultural obstacles and come ready with the solutions**. If you feel stuck in figuring out what those solutions look like, find the people in your field who have taken time away, ask around, and see if you can talk with them about how they did it.

For many people, a mini-retirement can kick off a new habit, lifestyle, or hobby. They want to take some of what they learned and develop it into their next job. If an employer thinks so poorly of the fact that you have people you care about outside of work, interests, goals, or hobbies, maybe they aren't the right fit for you. If the fact you took some time to focus on your life outside of your profession stirs up so much fear or hostility, it could be an insight into that company's culture.

Explaining your reason for wanting a career gap doesn't have to create anxiety. For most of my clients, their concerns were unfounded. People were so interested in the cool things they did that their sabbatical became a strength, making them a memorable candidate.

CHAPTER SEVEN

NEGOTIATE YOUR SABBATICAL

About half of my coaching clients really enjoy their job and being part of the company they work for. They like the work culture, their coworkers, and the type of work they are doing. They simply need some time away to focus on their personal life and dreams. Afterward, they would be very happy to pick up where they left off at work.

I can't count the number of times I've heard, *"Oh, in my company, there is no way I would get a leave of absence. They aren't set up for that. I've never heard of anyone making that happen."* Only to hear, after the first negotiation round: *"You won't believe this! They were way more open to the idea than I thought. We need to figure out some details, but I think it might happen!"* Don't discount this idea just yet and skip to the next chapter. If the alternative is putting in your two-week notice, you might have more options than you realize.

Helping my clients with work negotiations might be one of my favorite parts of coaching. Because most people are unfamiliar with negotiation and it makes them uncomfortable, just a few hours of planning and preparation can boost their skill level and confidence by 10×. That's my goal for you in this chapter. I'll show you a few best-practice frameworks that you can apply to all three types of negotiation that are helpful for mini-retirements: negotiating time away, negotiating an unusual work arrangement, and negotiating your exit from the company.

How much time can I ask for? If you only need one to three months, it's worth asking for a sabbatical. For longer career breaks, you might need to separate from the company. You can leave with the understanding that you will reapply when you finish your sabbatical.

Do I ask for paid or unpaid leave? If your company doesn't offer paid leave other than vacation time, you probably won't get paid time off. To make the HR logistics easier, some companies will offer 25% pay during your sabbatical, covering your health insurance and other automated deductions.

THE FOUR ELEMENTS OF NEGOTIATION

There are four elements of this negotiation.

1. **Anticipate and articulate the challenges:** It's your job to figure out all the ways this doesn't work for your boss or company and come up with solutions. Don't put that task on them; they are busy with their own jobs. Make sure you prepare ahead of time. I call it radical empathy: Really try to imagine how your boss will feel and the challenges they will see. Next up is articulating those challenges. This can seem counterintuitive. Why bring up the challenges and draw attention to them? A few reasons. One, it shows you have put thought into this. Two, it proves that you are willing to collaborate to make this work. Most people struggle to be honest about the challenges. By voicing what they are already thinking, you take that task off their shoulders and move the conversation along productively.

2. **Bring solutions:** There will be challenges to you leaving for a month or three months. You need to put some mental and emotional energy into figuring out those solutions. For example, knowing who on your team could take some of your workload. Or helping train a temp to cover for you. When you are thinking of challenges, try to anticipate the ones that are real sticking points that could derail the negotiation. Then, see if you could make a low-cost compromise that doesn't impact your mini-retirement much but solves the biggest issue.
3. **Collaborative and creative:** This is the attitude that you will bring to the negotiation. This isn't a threat or you being demanding. You aren't dumping this problem on their lap. You are going to try to work together to find creative solutions. You are open to their ideas, suggestions, and concerns. You show up prepared but flexible in your approach.
4. **It's a process:** These types of negotiations will take time. Any time you ask for something unusual, your boss will have to have additional meetings with other people, either their bosses, HR, or other teams. You need to be patient. Demanding that you get everything you want by the end of the first meeting is unrealistic. If those are the terms, the answer will be no. Set the expectation for a time frame of a few weeks or months. If the time frame is longer than six months, you will make zero progress until the month before.

HEADS-UP EMAIL

Don't launch a sneak attack. No matter which type of negotiation you are planning, send a heads-up email when you request a meeting with your boss. When people are shocked, surprised, or scared, it spikes their cortisol. This natural stress response helps you concentrate on small details but is awful at helping people see the big picture, think creatively, and find unique solutions. The heads-up email should be short and sweet; no need to share your master plan. But it gives them a context for the conversation that's about to happen.

Here are two examples:

> "Hey Sara, I'm hoping we can set up a time to chat next week. I have some personal plans that I'm trying to figure out, and I'd love to discuss a potential leave of absence. Is there a time that works best for you?"

> "Hi Henry, I hope you had a great vacation. After you get settled in, I'd love to find a time to talk. I have some summer plans that need some extra time away from work. You know how much I love working here, so hopefully we can find a way to make it work. When's a good time?"

STAGES OF GRIEF

The heads-up email serves two functions. The first, as I mentioned, is that it helps your boss mentally prepare and be less surprised. The second purpose is that it gives them time to move through the stages of grief.

It might be odd to think about your boss grieving because you're embarking on a mini-retirement. But your absence will create a change, a loss, and challenges. The first stage of grief is denial. The *"Well, this just can't happen."* Then comes anger. They might be frustrated that you will make their work life a bit harder by leaving. When your chat rolls around, you want them firmly in the bargaining stage. It will get them into a creative and collaborative mindset. By giving them a bit of heads-up and at least a few days to mentally prepare, you increase your chances of a productive conversation.

THE FIRST CONVERSATION

Now it's time for that first conversation. You will use the classic **sandwich method**. Good news, bad news, good news. The first part of the sandwich will be how much you enjoy your work, the company, and the people. Then, you share the bad news with your story about why you want to take this time off. Include as many of the mini-retirement story elements as possible: positive, interesting, specific, one-time event, and time-sensitive. Then you finish the sandwich with how excited you'll be to return. Explain how you want to stay with the organization, and see a lot of future growth here. You hope that you can figure out a way to make that happen.

Here are two examples of what that could sound like.

> *"Thanks so much for taking the time to meet with me. As you know, I'm excited about the kinds of projects I've been working on lately. Working for this company has been amazing, from the incredible coworkers to the culture. I'm hoping we can figure out a way for me to take an extra four unpaid weeks off. You see, my mom is really into cycling. She and my dad always dreamed of cycling across Europe when they retired. Her last day of work is in four months. But my dad passed away a year ago. I would love to help her make that dream come true. We would spend six weeks cycling through Croatia and Northern Italy. It's a once-in-a-lifetime trip for sure. And it would be an incredible experience to share with my mom while she is still fit and healthy. I will have two weeks of paid leave I can use, but I would need another four weeks unpaid to make this adventure happen. I've really loved working here. I see so much potential for growth at the company*

over the next few years. I'd love to work with you to figure out a plan. I have some ideas."

Or:

"I appreciate you meeting with me. I've had such an amazing experience working at the company so far. I feel like I've really found my place here. I'm hoping we can figure out how I can take a three-month sabbatical. I've always dreamed of planting a food forest in my backyard. Over the years, I've tinkered and done what I can to get it started. I plan to take the summer and go all in to set it up. I plan to plant 20 trees and over a hundred bushes, plus building raised beds, a pond, and a patio. If I have the time this summer, I could knock it all out and then just enjoy the literal fruits of my labor for the rest of my life. But if I keep plugging away on the weekends, it might take me 20 years. I've enjoyed working here so much and feel like we have a great group of people. I'm excited to see if there is any way we can work this out so I can fulfill this dream and stay at a job I love."

THE LEVERAGE OF LEAVING

The willingness to leave isn't good leverage because it's a threat or punishment. It's not leverage because you get to stomp off if you don't get your way.

The willingness to leave is good leverage because it changes the equation. You taking a mini-retirement or negotiating a new work role is inconvenient. The easiest option for your boss or company is for nothing to change. With one word, "No," they have saved themselves a bunch of hassle. You stay working the same role, day in and day out. Because people often choose the simplest and easiest path, if they can say no and nothing changes, they will usually say no.

Changing the equation means it's easier, faster, and cheaper to give you the requested time off than replace you. That's what you have to set out to prove. How can you make your time off easier, faster and cheaper than replacing you would be?

You can lightly sprinkle this into the conversation. Simply add one line to this conversation opener. If there is a lot of resistance, you can be more heavy-handed later in the conversation.

For example:

> *"I'd hate to give up my position here, so I'm really hoping we can work something out."*

> *"You know how much I would miss working here; I'd love to find a way to come back."*

> *"This dream is really important to me. I would prefer not to separate from the company. This has been a wonderful job."*

I've had clients in various industries and workplaces, including big corporations, healthcare, government jobs, small businesses, law firms, insurance companies, construction companies, accountants, and salespeople. As such, I've heard every type of resistance.

> *"My company isn't touchy-feely. They really don't care about my happiness."*

> *"My boss doesn't respect me or even understand what I do. Plus, they are all a bit low-key racist."*

> *"I have too much responsibility to leave."*

"My role is unique and really hard to replace."

"I'm the only person at my company who does what I do. There isn't anyone to cover for me."

"There are no exceptions to policy. No one has ever done this."

While it's true that every company and industry has its own unique challenges, 95% of companies have this trait in common: they are run by people, and people generally go with the easiest, cheapest, and quickest solution. Your mini-retirement is the best solution for everyone. Now prove it.

ACCOMMODATING IS EASIER AND CHEAPER

For anyone who has taken courses on employee hiring or retention, a lot is said about the cost of hiring and training new employees. Not to mention the lost revenue or productivity as that new hire slowly gets up to speed in their role. Retention is almost always the cheaper and easier route, even when accommodations need to be made. When hiring someone new, there is also the risk that they won't be as good as you. They might be missing key skill sets, knowledge, or soft skills that make the workplace more productive. People often want to stay with the known vs the unknown. In this case, you are the known. Whoever they might find to replace you is the unknown.

As these conversations progress, you can highlight how returning to work, despite the short absence, is still less effort and a lower-risk option than replacing you. I met Ben at an event I was speaking at about mini-retirements. He said because he was an executive, there was little chance of him getting extended time away; he was simply too important. That's one way to look at it. But perhaps there is a more helpful way to view this situation.

I asked, "How much time off would you hope to take?"

He said, "Honestly, if I could just get a month off, I feel like I could finally get some rest and clear my head."

"OK," I said, "and how long would it take for them to find a replacement for your role, start to finish?"

"Oh, geesh," he said, "that's a six-month process."

I smiled a bit. "How long would it take a new hire to get up to speed?"

"Another six months minimum."

"OK," I said, "so which choice is easier, giving you a month off or taking six months to interview and hire a new executive? Plus, six months for that person to get up to speed and produce like you do now?"

People often view having a critical role in a company, or possessing deep industry knowledge, as a reason they would never be granted time off. In reality, those factors make it more costly and time-consuming to replace you. I once met an executive from Starbucks who, when he started, was told by another executive, "It'll take a year before you even understand your job." He scoffed at the time because he had a lot of experience with this type of work. But he told me, "You know what? They were right. I was still figuring out my role a year into it."

There will be challenges to you taking an extended time away. But if you do some work up front and position it as the easier, cheaper, and quicker choice, your request will be granted more often than not. If people still feel indispensable, I'll ask them, "What would they do if you had a heart attack or learned you had cancer and needed three months to recover? Has anyone ever taken leave to have a baby?" The answer is that the company would have to figure it out. Your sabbatical will create a bit of stress and inconvenience, but less than you leaving for good. If you are "indispensable," preparing for your absence will also create a more resilient organization—and maybe more appreciation when you return.

KNOW YOUR VALUE REPLACEMENT

One of the areas you can prepare for this negotiation is to map out and understand your professional contribution and the value you bring to the team. Sometimes, clients will resist this because they assume their boss should understand their role and the value they bring to the team. Reality doesn't always rise to meet our expectations. If you are part of a small team, maybe your direct manager knows 80%. Perhaps the manager above them understands 60% of what your role entails and the value you provide. Those numbers go down quickly if you are part of a large team. When I managed coffee shops, I had teams of 25–40 employees. I tried to put way more effort than average into understanding my employees, their contributions, and their areas for professional growth. But that's a lot of people to keep track of when people's contributions and performance constantly change.

It's best not to leave this to chance. Assume they are humans who aren't entirely focused and attuned to your contribution, knowledge, skill set, and all the value you bring. It's like that line when a couple breaks up, *"He doesn't even know how good he had it."* And there is often truth to that saying. not just in love but also in work. Your boss probably doesn't know all the ways you contribute and how big a gap you would leave if you separated from the company. Take the time to outline your contributions.

CHAPTER SEVEN

MAKE CONCESSIONS

I once had a coworker who dreamed of going to Paris. She had everything planned out in her head: the fanciest hotels, gourmet restaurants, all-day shopping trips to designer stores. I asked if she had ever been to France.

"No, not yet. I'm waiting until I can afford my dream trip," she replied.

"Well," I started, "a simpler trip could still be fun. I've done some really budget trips there and had a blast. It could at least give you a little taste of the city."

Nope, it was all or nothing. She would rather never see Paris than compromise on her dream trip. It can be easy to get stuck in all-or-nothing thinking. Either you get to do your perfect adventure for the exact length of time and forget all about work... or you pout and skip the whole thing.

When you think about the challenges to your leaving, which ones have no clear solution? The responsibilities no one can imagine how they would be handled without you. Maybe you can make a small concession and resolve the most significant issues.

For example, one of my clients was an accountant at a small company. She picked a slow season for her three-month mini-retirement. She could help onboard and train a temp to cover most of her tasks. The most significant sticking point was the end-of-the-month books. That was something they wouldn't trust to a temp. Her solution was to come in at the end of each month for a day. It didn't interfere with her plans or vacations. Going in for three days when she could get the whole summer off was an easy solution for both parties.

If you're the point person for a big account, maybe you can still be available for those meetings during your time off. Perhaps you could check your email twice a week. Or call in via Zoom for the Friday team meeting. Whatever that one big thing is that makes your manager think, *"How in the world can we figure this element out?"* Maybe you can offer a small compromise that doesn't significantly impact your mini-retirement. The goal is to recognize the things that could be deal breakers or pain points for the organization, but where a compromise is palatable for you. High value for them, low cost to you.

If your company has never given someone a leave of absence, perhaps no one ever came in with this game plan. Maybe no one took the time to prepare. This preparation isn't a huge time commitment; with just four to six hours, you will massively increase your odds of success.

CHAPTER EIGHT
EXIT NEGOTIATION

MY CLIENT SEEMED concerned when we started planning her exit negotiation. She asked the question slowly, making sure she understood the details, "So you're saying that when I put in my notice, I should *ask for a raise*? In the same conversation? Is that even a thing people do?"

Maybe you have decided to separate from your company for mini-retirement, either because you are sure they won't give you the time off, you want a longer career break, or you aren't interested in returning to the company. Your current plan is to give your notice, pack up your desk, and that's it. Then you move on to the next chapter of your life.

Before you put in your notice for your mini-retirement, consider an **exit negotiation**. An exit negotiation is a separation plan that smooths your transition out of the company to benefit you and your employer. What are the ways you could help the company prepare for your exit, and are there things you would appreciate in return?

My client was excited about her upcoming mini-retirement but knew her employer would never grant her the time off. Instead, we starting crafting her exit negotiation. She was highly doubtful that she could secure a raise while putting in her notice. The exit negotiation looked like this: she would stay on for four months during their busiest and most important season for her work. She would then help find and train her replacement. After her separation from the company, she would be available periodically. In *return*, she would appreciate being fairly compensated until she left. She had done her market research and found that fair compensation was about 20% higher than she was currently being paid for her position.

"Fair" is a powerful word in negotiation. Very few people want to be seen as being unfair or unreasonable. She listed all of the ways in which she was willing to help the company with this transition, and in exchange, she was simply asking to be *fairly* compensated. The company's owners seemed extremely grateful for all the consideration she was willing to make and happily granted her the 20% raise.

HOW CAN YOU ADD VALUE?

When planning your exit, think through all of the ways to make your exit easier and smoother for the company. This is especially helpful for people who hold more senior roles, integral roles, or positions that can be challenging to fill.

What would be helpful to make it an easy, smooth exit out of your company? This might be a longer time frame for your notice. During this time, you could help interview and train your replacement. You could offer to go part time towards the end to make the transition easier. Consider what you're willing to give. What are the things that aren't a huge cost to you that you would be willing to do anyway, and would be extremely beneficial for your company?

> **How much notice should you give?** If you hold a lot of responsibility that isn't easily passed to coworkers, or it will take time to find your replacement, start the conversations about four months before you would like to exit. Most companies try to postpone change for as long as possible.

In return, what are things that you would appreciate? Some of the things that I've seen clients be able to negotiate are full vesting of benefits ahead of schedule. Bonuses to be paid out ahead of time or after their separation. Raises to bring them up to fair compensation. Being able to work remotely as they transition out of the company. A shorter or adjusted schedule that helps them ease into their mini-retirement.

IN RETURN, I'D APPRECIATE

The phrasing that is the most successful goes like this: *"I would be happy to ABC, in return I would appreciate XYZ."* These exit negotiation requests aren't threats or demands. You'll take the same creative and collaborative approach as with all of our other negotiations. You want to create a plan that's mutually beneficial. This is often seen as extremely fair and reasonable. It's harder for an employer to say I want you to make all of these concessions so the transition is easier on my end, but I'm not willing to give you any of the things that you're asking for.

There are non-financial benefits as well. A thoughtful exit leaves you in better standing with your co-workers and boss. You'll be seen as generous and thoughtful. If you have a strong relationship with your co-workers and perhaps feel a little bit of guilt about your exit, knowing that you're doing everything you can to make the transition as easy as possible for everyone can ease some of that guilt. It also gives you a better chance of keeping the door open to be rehired in the future or to securing good recommendations.

Of course, there are jobs that we want out of as fast as possible and bosses we hope never to see again. A quick and simple notice fits the bill in those cases. But if you like your company, thinking through all the ways you can make this transition easier for the company and also beneficial to you is worth the time and effort.

CHAPTER NINE

NEGOTIATE THE UNUSUAL

When I started working with Jamie a few years ago, she faced a common challenge for people advanced in their careers. In her 50s, she wasn't sure she wanted to spend the next ten years in this field, but wasn't financially ready to retire. She knew she needed a break but wasn't sure if she wanted to return to her current career or try out a whole new profession that potentially wouldn't pay as well.

If you can improve the job you already have, it gives you a chance to see if you want to stay with your current company after your mini-retirement. Over the years, I've helped lots of clients negotiate unusual work situations. Things that initially seemed out of the realm of possibility. In reality, using some of the techniques and ideas that we've already discussed, most workplaces are more flexible than we imagine. Companies will typically opt for the easiest and simplest solution when choosing between losing a good employee or making some accommodations. Often, the accommodations become possible.

This was especially true in Jamie's position. She worked in an industry that required deep knowledge of the subject matter. To be effective in her position, a candidate would need a minimum of ten years of experience in that field, preferably 15. And with the industry workforce aging and retiring, the pool of candidates was getting smaller each year. At a minimum, it took about six months to find a suitable replacement for her role.

Here are a few examples of what I've seen over the years:

- People being able to work part time.
- 80% work schedule at 80% pay.
- Remote work.
- Switching employment status from W2 to a more flexible contract position.
- Designing entirely new roles.

People with seasonal hobbies, like downhill skiing in the winter or hiking in the summertime, can create flexible roles where they work more in a demanding work season and then have more free time to enjoy their hobbies during the low season. As you grow your financial freedom, you have more options in the types of roles you can accept.

After a few sabbaticals, many people love the lifestyle flexibility of alternating between periods of work and leisure. They often find or create unique jobs that easily allow them to retire often.

> One of my podcast guests had taken a sabbatical every summer while his kids were young, allowing them to travel extensively. When his wife was recruited by a former employer to join a new company, her one non-negotiable was a month off every summer. Her boss said, "Done," and she never had to negotiate a mini-retirement again. It's a win for her because it allows for their ideal lifestyle. And a win for her employer because she has little reason to leave.

As unlikely and complicated as it may seem, I've had several clients design entirely new roles in a company. Having specific deep knowledge of the workings of a company and seeing the areas of opportunity, they can create roles that utilize most of their strengths while avoiding most of their weaknesses. They can solve challenging issues that the company hasn't figured out how to solve before.

There are three simple steps to prepare for this negotiation.

1. **Personal assessment.** Create an assessment of all of your unique strengths, your skill set, and your personality. Similar to what we've done in other exercises before a negotiation, but in this one, I want you to think more broadly. What things come more naturally to you? What things are you just four times better at doing than the average bear?
2. **Identify challenges.** The next step is to consider your company's needs and challenges. This is ideal to do after you've been there for at least a year, preferably a couple of years, and understand the ins and outs. In every company, small parts of the business just don't work very well. There could be a seasonality to the work where the workload increases past the employees' capabilities for a few months a year. There could be a set of responsibilities that doesn't exactly fall on one person's plate and always gets shuffled around and never done well. Maybe there aren't more upper-level positions that don't involve directly managing people, so it creates a stalling point for those wanting to advance but for whom managing others isn't their strongest suit. It might be a small piece of workload that, while it doesn't need a full-time employee, doesn't exactly fit into other people's job descriptions or skills.
3. **The ask.** Then, think about what you really want from your work role. Are there changes that would be incredibly helpful to you and also benefit the company? What would a unique arrangement look like? How could it make your boss's life easier? How would it solve the challenges? Would it save the company money or increase profit?

Just like in the other types of negotiation, you will organize all of this information and devise a loose plan framework. Many of the same principles apply. You don't have to have every detail sorted out; instead, bring that same creative, collaborative approach to the process. This will also be a negotiation that might take a couple of meetings and a bit of time to sort out. If it's a simple request like working more remotely or making sure you can leave the office by 4:00 p.m., you might be able to sort that out in one or two meetings. This process averages one to two months for more complicated requests like designing an entirely new work role in your company.

Jamie decided to try her hand at creating an entirely new work role to experiment and see if that would help her enjoy the rest of her career. The role she designed helped solve a couple of problems in the company. One being that there weren't more advanced roles that didn't involve managing people, so some people were stuck in their career progression. The second problem this new role solved was having someone with more experience available to help other team members. It took a few months to create the role, but as she settled into this new role, she found it a lot more enjoyable and fulfilling.

As you begin these conversations, you'll start with the same heads-up email we've used before. You want to give a bit of context for what the meeting is about. This doesn't need to be longer than three sentences. It might sound something like this, for example:

> *"I'd love to catch up later this week or perhaps next week. I have a couple of ideas about ways we could make some shifts in my work role to solve the issue of XYZ. Is there a good time that works for you?"*

CHAPTER NINE

Or:

"I'm hoping we can set up a meeting for some time next week. I've had a few responsibility shifts in my personal life and, thinking through my current role, I'd love to explore the possibility of trying an 80% workload for a period of time. Is there a time that's best for you?"

You want to show that you've put a good deal of time as well as mental and emotional energy into making this the best possible scenario for everyone. This isn't something you can flop on your boss's plate and expect them to figure out for you.

You'll want to create a **test time frame** for this change. Something that gives both parties a clear exit point if it's not working very well. The company will be far more hesitant to allow an exception or change if they feel locked into it forever. For example, with the 80% workload, you could ask for that to span no more than four months. A longer time frame is more appropriate when creating a whole new position in a company. Six months to a year allows everyone to see the benefit this position brings and how well it's working out.

BENEFITS OF A CUSTOM JOB

There are three important benefits to creating a unique work situation. First, it makes your work easier or more enjoyable until you start your sabbatical. Between an easier work situation and the knowledge that the sabbatical will happen eventually, people feel more at peace with their current situation.

Secondly, it gives you some time to prepare for your mini-retirement financially. You might be able to create an arrangement that makes it feasible to stay for another year. This also gives you the runway and mental space to plan your mini-retirement. You can practice some of the habits or activities you have planned for your time off. You can research and plan for your adventure during this in-between time.

The third big benefit, frequently underestimated, is that once you become the exception to the policy and create something unique, you are exponentially more likely to negotiate an exception to the policy in the future successfully. When your boss and your company see how well you're able to perform in unique and new positions, and how you're able to form something that increases productivity, it creates trust that you can handle other unique new roles in the company. You become the outlier who doesn't need the same rules to be productive.

Jamie stayed in this new role for almost a year. At that point, while she was really enjoying her new work role, she decided it was time to either quit or take a sabbatical. We started coaching sessions again to help her negotiate this exit. I always want clients to be mentally and emotionally prepared for various offers or situations that their boss might suggest in this bargaining stage. Although she assured me that part time would never be possible in her company, I still wanted her to be mentally prepared ahead of time in case that interested her. While negotiating her resignation, her boss asked if she would be willing to stay on for four months part time to help ease the transition. This was a perfect situation for her. It would allow her to ease into her mini-retirement, slowly scaling up her active rest, relationships, and hobbies while maintaining income that would help cover her bills. She had thrived being the exception before, and they were eager for her to be the exception again.

CHAPTER TEN

BEFORE YOU GO, AND FINDING THE NEXT JOB

WHEN I TALK to people about retiring often, being able to find the next job is consistently one of their top concerns. The funny thing is, with just the tiniest amount of preparation, most people's actual experience is the opposite of concerning. They find themselves with too many job offers, and people in their network trying to pull them out of their mini-retirement sooner than planned.

When Adam left his 9–5 job to take a year off, multiple people soon recommended jobs or informally made job offers. Oddly enough, he never received unsolicited job offers while employed. Why, in his year away from work, were people coming out of the woodwork to find him a job? Some of this can be explained by a few best practices that we will go over, but there is a bigger force at play—our modern work obsession.

MODERN WORK CULTURE

When you meet someone at a party and they ask *"What do you do?"*, they aren't asking about your hobbies or how you have fun with your friends. They don't really want to know about your passion and hidden expertise. They are asking about your employment.

Work is so closely tied to our identities. As kids, we are asked, *"What do you want to be when you grow up?"* People mean what you want to do professionally—but make it sound like your very essence. What you will *be*. It is as though our being a son, friend, traveler, book reader, or cook isn't part of our identity.

Work culture also creates strong ties between employment and morality. To choose not to work is seen as lazy. The phrase *"people just don't want to work"* gets thrown around. It's said as a criticism. The implication is that people are selfish, lazy, or unwilling to do their part to make the economy run, or at least keep the doors of Taco Bell open for when we want a late-night snack.

This work culture runs especially strong in some professions where lack of personal life supposedly proves commitment to your work. Do you even *care* if you aren't bankrupting your personal life to make professional progress?

The emphasis on work culture can be seen in families as well. My work with clients has shown me that in some communities, like second- or third-generation Southeast Asian families, it's sometimes especially prominent. The currency their parents trade within their social circle can be professional success, even more so than wealth. It matters less that their daughter is a millionaire with a great lifestyle; 90% of the bragging rights fall onto the profession. Doctor. Lawyer. Engineer.

There are strong cultural forces that will work against you when you try to step away to carve out time to focus on things that matter to you. Fortunately, these same forces will provide momentum to pull you back into the workforce.

You being unemployed makes people uncomfortable. Consciously or unconsciously, your friends, family, old coworkers, and professional network will be slightly uncomfortable knowing you are out there in the world... not working. Even if you provide no encouragement or guidance, they will try to pull you back into the workforce to ease their own discomfort.

Your mini-retirement opens a mental loop in people's minds, and they will continually search for ways to close that loop. One of my clients, Mary, decided to take a year off. She really wanted to protect this time off, so she didn't do everything we will discuss in this chapter to encourage job offers. Nevertheless, within two weeks, people were coming out of the woodwork to find her a new job. The neighbor she chatted with while going on her morning walk had a cousin whose non-profit was hiring. Other departments at her old job were wondering if she might join them. Friends and family were trying to make connections with work opportunities. Despite clear and firm boundaries protecting this time away, the connections and offers kept coming.

It's human nature in a work culture society. Even if you don't want it, it's inevitable to some degree. In this chapter, I want to show you how to lean into this natural phenomenon to find more interesting, better-suited, and better-paying work after your mini-retirement.

> You stepping away from your career will illicit three reactions from coworkers.
>
> 1. A few people will be genuinely interested in your time off and be happy for you.
> 2. Some will be confused. Perplexed by your motivation, the financials, or the logistics.
> 3. And people will be angry. How dare you leave this system they have based their entire purpose and identity on? We will talk about how to communicate with this type of coworker in Step Four.

NETWORKING

Networking is a bit like the tree parable. The best time to plant a tree was ten years ago, and the second best time is today. The best time to be intentional and thoughtful in networking was ten years ago. The second best time is today.

The idea of networking is often uncomfortable for people. It feels transactional and kind of cheesy. That style of networking was never going to work for me. As an introvert by nature, a big networking mixer with lots of banter and passing out business cards makes me nauseous to even think about. You're more likely to find me hyperventilating behind a fake plant than wheeling and dealing in social currency. Bless you if you're a social butterfly who sparkles in a room and draws all the attention—that's fewer eyes on me. But perhaps there is a different mental framework that can work for the rest of us.

Networking for introverts

Several years ago, I gave a talk at a huge conference of personal finance media. I titled it "Networking for Introverts." In a conference full of writers and content creators, who are often introverts, it was a very full room. A lot of us struggle with the concept of networking. We know it's important, but how do we do it in a way that feels authentic and fits our personality?

My premise for networking for introverts is that it is about **relationships**. Real relationships, not transactional ones. Investing in those relationships not only enhances our professional lives but can be a source of support when needed.

In the massively popular book, *The 5 Love Languages*, Gary Chapman outlines five ways that people give and receive love. Touch, words of affirmation, gifts, quality time, and acts of service. This is a very helpful framework to consider when investing in professional relationships. You never know what someone's love language might be or what will be meaningful to them. Recently, I spoke at an event that I have spoken at a few times before. The event organizer mentioned how he often thinks about the first time I was a speaker there because I brought him a gift. That was years ago now. But he said that, out of the dozens of speakers he has had over the years, I was only one of two that ever brought a gift for him. I can't remember what the gift was. I'm sure it wasn't expensive or even very specific to him. But the gift mattered.

In my professional circle, I try to invest in my relationships with all five love languages. I buy people gifts. I send cards and emails with words of affirmation. If they need help, I'm there with an act of service. If they need to talk, I'll spend quality time, even if it's just over Zoom. While "touch" can be tricky in professional circles, I try to at least maintain warm body language. A handshake, a pat on the back, or, in some cases, a hug can show a closeness of relationship.

In every industry, your opportunities are different. I'm self-employed and don't live near any of my professional friends. I make sure to connect on social media, email, calls, by attending events and conferences, and meeting up if I'm in their town. A few years ago, I sent about a hundred holiday cards and gifts to my professional friends. To me, that represented years of building those relationships and an incredible group of friends.

Make sure you are there when it matters. My motto is: *the right gift at the right time for the right reason.* In celebration, mourning, and times of change, make sure you show up. A card, text, a gift, or a call. When they get promoted, take on a new big project, switch jobs, get laid off, a parent passes away, or a child is born.

If you have never put any thought or intention into cultivating your professional relationships, try to start some new habits before you leave your job, at least three to six months before your mini-retirement. You'll need to practice ways to stay in touch with colleagues outside of the office or workgroup chats once you're gone.

For me, the best networking is about investing in relationships. When the time comes for some help or support, you have a group of friends who can help. Often, it's not that group directly, but they can connect you with their own networks of friends.

RETIRE OFTEN

THE GOODBYE EMAILS

There are two goodbye emails that you can send when it's time to separate from your job. The first is the standard and obligatory email. This is where you let people inside and outside of your organization know when your last day of work is and who the new point of contact is.

The only small addition would be one or two personal lines to include that will help open the mental loop that you are available for new work projects. The email might sound something like this.

> "I wanted to inform you that my last day of work is XXX. From that point forward, XXX will be able to help you, and this is their email and phone number XXX."

Then add this as a small addition to the mass email that is often sent out as part of your transition out of the company:

> "It has been an amazing experience working for XXX company. After my sabbatical, I hope our paths cross again in the future."

Or:

> "I have really enjoyed working at XXX these last X years. I'm excited for my upcoming mini-retirement, but looking forward to new and interesting roles in [this industry] in the future."

There is a second email that you can send to those you are closer to, either in your company or your larger professional network. Depending on the work culture, these might be combined. In the second email, you add more context for your leaving, as well as opening that mental loop that you are open to new work in the future. It can sound something like this.

CHAPTER TEN

"I wanted to inform you that my last day of work is XXX. From that point forward, XXX will be able to help you, and this is their email and phone number XXX. I have really enjoyed working with you all. My time at XXX company has been incredibly rewarding. I am planning on taking a six-month mini-retirement. I have many fun adventures planned for my time away, including [add one or two big things here: working on a book, hiking Kilimanjaro, training for a triathlon, a road trip with the family]. But I'm also excited about what the next chapter in my professional life will look like. I hope that we have the chance to work on projects again in the future. While I have many plans for my time away, if you happen to hear of anything that would be a perfect fit for me, feel free to reach out. I'd love to stay in touch. The best way to reach me is XXX. Thank you all so much for making these last XXX years so rich with professional growth for me."

Word will still get around if you don't email to explain your sabbatical. It's best to control the narrative as you exit. When Adam left his last 9–5 job, he sent both emails to coworkers and professional contacts outside the company. But the idea of someone simply taking a year off to focus on other things seemed incredibly unlikely. Soon, a rumor started floating around that he wasn't really taking time away from work. Instead, this whole thing was a ruse to keep his coworkers in the dark until the company announced his new promotion. He had given a long notice, and as his remaining time drew to a close, there were several very confused coworkers. Some of the questions were explicit. *"Wait, you really are leaving? You don't have another job lined up? You're actually just taking a career break?"* And then there were a host of implied questions that were skirted around. *"Who does this? How can you afford to take a year off?*

Did you win the lottery?" Well, maybe they weren't thinking that last one, but that would have made more sense.

STAY TOP OF MIND

If you want to help secure new and hopefully better employment at the end of your mini-retirement, you can encourage that natural desire people will have to see you back in the workforce by staying top of mind. As part of your preparation for leaving, you hopefully found ways to connect with your professional network outside of the office and work channels. You'll want to devote some time to maintaining those relationships when you are gone. You can use what works well for you—perhaps email, social media, lunches, or still attending professional events. You can also add some new ways to stay connected.

During his first year off, Adam would drop into one of his old workplaces every few months with a box of donuts. It was an old-fashioned workplace with a water cooler and coffee pot in the break room where people would congregate. He would let his coworkers know he was still enjoying his mini-retirement but was interested in new professional opportunities in the future. As a result, when positions opened up, someone would reach out or mention it to him when we ran into each other at community events.

Continuing to invest in your relationships keeps you top of mind. When people sit around in meetings and think about who could be a good addition to the team, your name will pop up. When your old college friend is bemoaning that they need to hire a new person, they will mention you as a possible solution.

Several years ago, I met Bob at an event I was speaking at. He was considering retiring early but was hesitant at the finality of that choice. Instead, I suggested he take a year off and see how it goes. It would be easier to explain to friends, family, and coworkers. Plus, it would give him an easy out in case this early retirement didn't work out. He now jokes that he is three years into a one-year mini-retirement. Even this far removed from his old career, he still gets calls from former coworkers. *"Bob, we have this new project coming, and buddy, it has your name written all over it!"* His response is still, *"No, it really doesn't have my name on it. But thanks for thinking of me."*

The upside of work culture is that if you take a few of these steps, your network might bring you work options that are more lucrative, a better fit, or offer a better work-life balance. Preferably all three.

CHAPTER ELEVEN
SELF-EMPLOYED

After publishing my first book, I knew a season of rest would be needed. I wrote it in 2020 while moving homes and tackling a full house remodel. By the time I finished editing, publishing, and promoting, I was ready for a break. The pattern of intense work followed by intense rest is one that is familiar and comforting to me. Adam and I set out on a three-month adventure with the family, traveling across the country in our camper. Unfortunately, the recovery process doesn't always fit into the timelines we give it. Sure, I felt much better when I arrived home. But I had the nagging feeling I wasn't 100%. I planned out my next projects and tried to get back into the swing of things. I rallied my team for the big plans I had. Despite the hype I was trying to sell myself, I still hadn't recovered. I needed more time. Creative energy is a tricky thing. When you run low, you run low. You can try to push through, but that doesn't fill the empty well.

Reluctantly, I made the hard call that my three-month mini-retirement was actually going to be a year-long one. The response to this announcement was split into two categories. My 9–5 employee friends gushed about how lucky I was to have that flexibility, which is true. My entrepreneur and business friends were more cautious because they understood the challenging logistics of such an endeavor.

The reality is that when you own a business, it's more complicated to take time off. It seems like it should be easier. You're the boss, and you can just give yourself permission. Who can say no? It's not like they can fire you.

Having walked dozens of employees and business owners

through this process of preparing for a mini-retirement, it's much more logistically challenging to take time away from something you have created. While it's never emotionally easy to walk away from the 9–5, it's technically simple. You put in your notice, have a few conversations, and spend a few weeks to a few months handing your role over to someone else and off you go! As the saying goes, *"Not my circus, not my monkeys."* Well, as a business owner, this is your circus, and these are your monkeys.

That being said, if you put in the time and effort to redesign your business, it can become more similar to the dream gig people imagine it to be. This won't be a one- or two-month project like leaving the 9–5. In my experience, most business owners need at least six to 12 months to really prepare their business and employees to manage without them. As a business owner, you will most likely make more concessions than the 9–5 employees. You don't want the place to burn to the ground while you are gone. You have put so much of your life into getting your business to this point. During my year hiatus, as I called it, I still worked five hours a week. Those couple of hours a week keep the wheels on, so I had something to return to.

REDESIGN OR SELL?

You have two choices. Sell your business or redesign it to run without you. You don't have to decide right away, although you might have a good inclination about how this will go. Either way, the beginning of the process is really similar, no matter which path you choose, because you need to be happy for this thing to function without you.

In *The 4-Hour Work Week*, Tim Ferriss talks about the crisis point in his business. He walked away feeling OK with it blowing up if it was going to blow up. I understand being at that point. If that's where you are, it's better for your business to blow up than for you to implode. But assuming you feel like you have some bandwidth and time to prepare, there are four areas of focus you should work on before you sell or begin your sabbatical.

Simplify. Automate. Document. Delegate.

These four steps are important in every organization where someone will be gone for a period of time. If you're an employee, there is something here for you as well as you prepare your coworkers to cover your duties. As a business owner, these four steps must happen, and you're the only one who can do it.

As we go through each one, I want to start by explaining why you probably haven't done this already, even though it benefits every business. Redesigning your business takes a good deal of work. There are logistics to figure out for sure. But there are a number of emotional stumbling blocks as well. You created this business, and extracting yourself so it runs without you isn't done without a few big feelings.

> **Spring cleaning.** Imagine these four steps are like spring cleaning your house. It's going to take time and effort. If might feel overwhelming or even messier while you're in the middle of the project. But at the end, your business, like your house, will be organized, decluttered, clean, and efficient. Business owners return to a smoother, easier job. You might find you have an extra ten hours a week of free time after your sabbatical. Some business owners funnel that into expansion. Some choose to prioritize their lifestyle post mini-retirement. Either way, your business will reward you for all the effort you put into this process, long after your sabbatical is finished. One of my newsletter

subscribers emailed me about how his wife works herself into a tizzy getting the house clean before they go on vacation. He said, it's like she wants their house to be ready to host their wake in case they die while on vacation. I'm sure Adam can relate. It's extra work upfront, but so nice to come home to a clean and organized home.

SIMPLIFY

There is often complexity in our business or work process. Because we are so familiar with the process, and quick to perform it, it's not a problem. Taking the steps to clean up the process would require much more work. And it's not really a priority because there haven't been many benefits until now. But if you want the freedom to step away from your role, you need to simplify the process so that other people can learn how to do it.

One of my clients had spent years running monthly reports manually, a task taking 15 minutes. Her new accountant set up a system where all the reports could be run automatically. Every business has those little glitches. Those things that take three minutes to do the "wrong" way or 90 minutes to fix forever. Your sabbatical is the perfect motivation to put in the extra effort to simplify your work process. It's additional upfront work, but you'll be rewarded with a more streamlined business when you return.

AUTOMATE

There are things you do every day, week, or month that are just easier to do than automate. You have the deep knowledge and experience to knock it out quickly. Setting up a process with guidelines for someone else to follow probably feels burdensome and less effective.

CHAPTER ELEVEN

How do you decide how much of this to order? How do you adjust staffing? What steps do you use to train new employees? There are things you do because it's easier, faster, and more effective to do it yourself. But underneath your intuition, there is a system working. Automation is about taking that internal system you instinctively follow and making it an external system others can utilize.

In this process, if you need help, recruit help. Maybe it's an employee, friend, or professional who can ask the right questions and help you understand why you are doing what you are doing that makes everything run so smoothly.

DOCUMENT

> Before you start the documentation process, keeping a **task journal** can be helpful. In it you make a note for each type of task you do. Depending on the nature of your work, this could be for a day, week, or month. This will give you an overview of which things need to be documented the most, what could be automated, simplified, or is able to be delegated. By doing this before you start, you can figure out which tasks to prioritize. You can also get feedback from the people who will be covering those tasks and understand which type of support is most useful for them.

I remember baking with my great grandma as a child. I was always curious about exactly how she did things. "How do you know how much salt to add?" I would ask as she tossed in a bit she had poured into her hand. "Oh, I just know. I've been making this for decades." Then, as a teenager, I was more aware of the fact that I would be moving away soon, and she might not be here forever to make my favorite dishes. "Can we write all this down? Can I measure everything as you make it so I know exactly how it's done?"

RETIRE OFTEN

I don't know if slowing down the process felt inconvenient, or maybe she assumed we would have hundreds more opportunities to capture these family recipes. Perhaps she wanted to be the one to always make these treats for me. Either way, a lot of the recipes I loved from childhood left with her.

Why do we resist documenting the process? I think we tell ourselves it's time-consuming and boring. And that's true. Maybe we assume there is a bit of magic that we add that just can't be written down. Because really, no one would be able to understand all the nuances like we do. Which might also be true. Do we fear being replaced? We hold the keys that make all this work. Why give away the secrets? There is a pull to be like my great grandma with her recipes.

At an event, I was talking to an employee of a company where the owners were all in their late 60s and planning on retiring soon. The problem was that no one else knew how to do their roles. These four steps—simplify, automate, document, and delegate—were all met with extreme resistance. This lady, very rightfully, was terrified she wouldn't have a job after the transition. If they refused to take the needed steps, all operations would quickly fall apart when they retired. There are obviously bigger things at play here. Why doom the very thing you have spent your life building? These four steps require a lot of effort, but it's in no way insurmountable.

Documentation is a pain. And I say this lovingly: if you need to hire a babysitter, do it. Someone to sit there and make you get it done is worth the investment. They can help with the documentation or just keep you accountable. There are consultants who specialize in this sort of thing. They will help you sort out which things need to be documented and the easiest way to go about it. It might feel overwhelming to you, but they have done this dance dozens of times.

CHAPTER ELEVEN

DELEGATE

Delegation is the thing everyone knows they should do, and everyone has a very good list of reasons why they can't or haven't. Logically, you know there must be someone in the world who could do at least part of your job, at least 80%, as well as you. Surely, there must be.

There are three stumbling blocks I see to making this happen.

The first is **frustration**. I once had a client who had repeatedly tried to find a babysitter for her five kids who met her standards. Exasperated, she said, "I don't know why it's so hard. I do this every day, all day. It's just a bit of cooking, light cleaning, playing with the kids, and helping them with schoolwork. Why can't I find anyone who can do a decent job at that?"

I just giggled. "You're joking, right? Do you really think anyone can do everything you do as well as you do it? You've been training your kids' entire life. You're the expert at this. If you can find someone who can do half of what you do, half as well, that's amazing."

It's frustrating that no one is you, isn't it? Why can't one person be everything you are, and preferably better? Why can't they seamlessly step in and create magic? Because they aren't you, and they can't; that's why. The sooner you realize this, the better off you'll be. I see so many business owners waiting for this fairytale person to come along. Occasionally, it happens. We have heard the stories. More often than not, it's a long, frustrating process with a lot of trial and error. Incredibly skilled recruiters specialize in finding CEOs and similar positions. They can spend six to 12 months searching and vetting the perfect replacement. Even then, it doesn't always work out. So the entire process starts over. It's frustrating.

The second thing is **waste**. I had a client who had basically given up on finding anyone who could help with any part of his job. At the core of his challenge, it was a fear of waste. He had wasted so much time, effort, and money in this pursuit. And he was no closer for it. How much more waste could he handle? He didn't have much hope it was even possible to find someone. Most small businesses don't have the resources to hire a specialty recruiter or add someone to their team who will make as much money as they do.

We worked on ways to minimize waste in the hiring and training process. Part of that was to let go of the expectation that one person could do his entire job exactly as well as he could. What parts of his job would be the easiest for another person to take over? Which parts were extremely high value but not too time intensive that he could maintain during his time away? He was OK working a few hours a week while he traveled with his family if it allowed him to take summers off.

The last stumbling block is **risk**. What if they mess something up? What if I trust someone and their underperformance is really detrimental to my business? I've found the first step to solving any problem is to be clear, specific, and honest about the problem. What exactly do you imagine happening? What is the worst-case scenario, and how does that play out? What kind of mistakes are most likely? Once you're clear on that, you can solve those problems. Create checks and balances, and a few fail safes.

At an event, I had a conversation with the founder and CEO of a company. She had just finished a year-long transition process utilizing a transition coach. Having worked with a few company founders, I was familiar with some of the stumbling blocks they face in separating. Knowing the answer, I jokingly asked, "So this transition coach is mostly tactical, or is there a good bit of therapy mixed in?" She laughed, "Oh honey, don't you know it." Preparing your business to run without you is a tactical and systems problem. But there are emotional and mental roadblocks as well. If you don't address the emotional or mental roadblocks, you'll never get through the tactical steps.

If you aim to maintain this business during your mini-retirement, it might look different from someone who walked away from a 9–5. There will be some small concessions. Maybe a few tasks that you maintain or double-check. You can still have 95% of the benefit of the mini-retirement with far less risk.

CHAPTER TWELVE

CALL ME CRAZY

I HAVE A CRAZY idea. Well, some people will think it's crazy. OK, most people will think it's crazy. They'll huff and puff and bemoan this new generation who cares about things other than work.

What if we made the last six chapters irrelevant? What if we reprinted this book in 30 years, and all of Step Two was removed. Ready for my wild idea?

What if we gave every employee a month off every year?

"But, but, but." I know. Call me crazy. I've worked for small businesses, big corporations and run my own business. I understand there are logistical challenges, cost factors, and productivity concerns. It would be hard. But we have proved we can do hard things. We have put people on the moon, created the internet, and given women the right to vote. We can figure out how to give people a month off. I'm sure of it. Hundreds of companies in the U.S. currently offer a sabbatical program, which is amazing. This crazy idea goes one step further.

Let's quickly look at two of the big challenges before I dive into the amazing benefits: cost and productivity. It's roughly 8%. Eight percent is one of 12 months. But it's really cost *or* productivity. You are losing one month's work, or 8% of your employees' work. (We will look at how it's unlikely even to be that high.) Or you are hiring someone else to cover that month's work. Essentially, for every 12 employees, you hire one extra, an 8% increase in cost. Either way, it's 8%. I pay all my freelancers a 10% bonus each year; so 8% isn't insurmountable in industries that pay well to attract talent.

The other challenge that's a knee-jerk reaction is the logistics. *"How will we ever pull this off?"* I don't want to be dismissive, but haven't you already done this? What if someone has a baby or suffers a heart attack? Aren't there systems in place for people to take more than two weeks off? It might take a bit of adjustment, but we aren't doing something HR has never attempted before.

Now that we have the cost-and-logistical elephant in the room acknowledged, I want you to pretend this is a magic trick. Suspend your disbelief for a few moments. Imagine this new way of business and work, and its benefits. Everyone taking a month off every year creates benefits not just for the employee but also for the company. There are probably a hundred benefits, but I want to highlight ten—and they're ones that any company can enjoy by implementing this kind of arrangement right now.

1. ATTRACT TALENT

In every industry, there are people who are head and shoulders above the rest. People who do 50% more than average or 50% better. Those people are hard to find and even harder to recruit. You need something unique and exciting to attract the best talent. Most people won't switch companies for a 10% raise, maybe not even a 20% raise. But a month off every year? That can transform the quality of their life much more than a 10% pay bump could.

2. SHARE INSTITUTIONAL KNOWLEDGE

A concern I hear is, *"Only Sarah knows how to do XYZ, so we couldn't possibly do without her for a month."* That challenge is actually an opportunity. Some people in your company hold these knowledge keys, and they aren't sharing. Maybe no one asked them to share, maybe no one has any motivation to learn what they do or maybe

Sarah doesn't want to share. But most likely, there just hasn't been a good reason to do the extra work of documenting and sharing that knowledge.

When everyone takes a month off every year, it creates an event that gives the motivation and deadline to document and share this industry knowledge. That way all the expertise doesn't get trapped in a few people.

3. CROSS-TRAIN TO BUILD RESILIENT TEAMS

In the process of capturing this institutional knowledge and sharing it, your team will be cross-training. A system is fragile when small breaks can collapse the whole thing. If your whole team or company would shut down if one person were gone for a month, you have a fragile system. By cross-training, you build a stronger and more resilient system because you are building in fail safes. If Sarah shares her knowledge between four different people, now there are backups if Sarah gets sick, or needs time off. Calling employees in the hospital with questions is never a good look and just proves you have built a fragile system. When everyone takes a month off every year, it forces cross-training to build flexible and resilient teams.

4. OPPORTUNITY FOR EMPLOYEE GROWTH

Due to cross-training and sharing of industry knowledge, new employees can gain expertise and experience. This gives a rare opportunity for employees to step into more senior roles and try their hand. Not only do they get the benefits of training, but they can test these roles to see if it's a direction they want to go with their career. Employees who can cross-train learn skills and experience that help them professionally, keep them engaged at the company, and prevent burnout or boredom. This also greatly benefits companies because they have a very simple and safe experiment to see where the promotion potential and talent lie. As an employer, you can see how people perform before you commit to a promotion. You can try people out in new roles, new teams, or even new departments. This makes succession planning more effective.

This further adds to creating flexible and resilient teams. If one team needs extra manpower for a busy season or project, you now have the ability to pull help from various parts of the company because they have temporarily filled these roles before.

5. MORE EQUALITY

Some of an employee's training, education, and growth happen during their on-the-job 9–5 hours. Yet a significant portion of professional growth occurs outside of typical work responsibilities for employees.

However, not every employee can take on this extra work after hours. People with extra family obligations, disproportionately women, are affected by this. When everyone takes a month off every year, you will help level the playing field in your organization.

Similar to a research sabbatical that professors might take, your employees have the ability to work on training or personal growth to further their careers. If women or minorities aren't progressing into leadership at the same rate, a month off every year can create more equality, by giving everyone the same opportunity to access job-related training to upskill their abilities.

CHAPTER TWELVE

6. RETENTION

After going through Step One, maybe you have imagined a bucket list with 20 incredible adventures. Even with a career break every five years, you would only get through five or six of those bucket list items. But imagine if you knew you would enjoy a month off every year at your company. You know next year is cycling across California. The year after, you are going to rebuild a car. In year three, your kids will be at the perfect age to take a month-long trip to Mexico, and learn Spanish as a family. Year four would be perfect for taking cooking classes with your mom in Rome because she will be retired by then. In year five, you'd love to buy a house and remodel it. You can envision all these incredible adventures laid out in front of you, year after year.

All you need to do? Be amazing at your job and stay at your company. You bring the dreams, and the company will help all these dreams come true by providing the time. *"A competitor will offer a $20,000 raise? That's great, but are you willing to give up all these dreams for some extra cash? What's more money if you can't enjoy life?"*

"But Jillian, if every company offers a month off every year, it won't be a benefit that will attract or retain talent." I'm an optimist and a visionary, but also a realist. Some CEOs would rather allow their companies to burn down than make paradigm-shifting changes that would help their employees. Only when faced with real pressure will change happen. It's simply too easy to keep things the same. I'll be thrilled if this becomes the norm in 50 years. The quicker you implement this radical sabbatical program, the longer you will have the competitive advantage.

7. WEED OUT LOW PERFORMERS

There are several valid reasons employees would resist taking a month off every month (an unfulfilling personal life, assuming no one can do their job as well as them, not wanting to burden the team, etc.). But another character might not want to take a month off: the low performer.

Are you ever baffled by how a coworker fills their time? They are around and sometimes look busy, but do they accomplish anything? They don't get fired because it's hard to prove they are massively inefficient with their time. Perhaps their supervisor is unaware of their performance. Maybe everyone just assumes that's how long the job takes.

All this comes to light when their workload gets divided up. Everyone knows exactly what they do and how long tasks should take. When they return, workload and expectations can be adjusted. Either the employee steps up, or the team can find a higher performer.

8. IMPROVE SOFT SKILLS

A high-quality advanced education will help prepare you for many aspects of your career. But five, ten, or 15 years into a career, it's evident it couldn't teach you everything. A month off doesn't have to be reserved for certifications and training. It can also be used to bolster these soft skills that could help an employee accelerate their performance. Maybe the weakness is leadership, communication, developing talent, public speaking, or time management. A good employee might have one or two weak spots that hold them back from becoming an exceptional employee.

CHAPTER TWELVE

9. IMPROVE PERFORMANCE

I don't think the 8% cost is really an 8% cost. For example, if you divide the job between lower-paid employees, that brings the true cost down. One factor that skews the 8% is that even with a week-long vacation, people work harder before they prepare to leave. And they work twice as hard to catch up when they return. It's one reason people don't use their vacation time—it's too stressful!

Diania, who negotiated a month off, is a great example. She was in sales and worked extra hard before and after her time off. She was already the top performer on the team, but that year she had the best sales year of her career, despite taking a month to hike the Camino. Preparing for a month off is still stressful but you are rewarded with a few weeks to truly relax. Employees come back to work more rested, creative, and energized from the time off, which is naturally more refreshing than a week-long vacation.

10. HELP PEOPLE DO HARD JOBS

Some jobs are hard. There is no way around it. My dad served multiple consecutive deployments in the Middle East with the Army. Living in a desert where people are actively trying to kill you and your friends every day is a tough gig. My mother might have a harder job. She is a teaching assistant for special needs children. The amount of patience, creativity, and energy it takes to handle those behaviors while giving kids a safe and supportive environment is incredible. She deserves the Nobel Peace Prize. And her pay is an insult to the incredible talent she brings.

How do you convince people to do insanely difficult work and keep them motivated, especially when the pay is laughable compared to the circumstances? Time off.

If you work in an industry that asks an unreasonable amount of your employees and you can't pay them half a million dollars, give them a month off every year. Take a lesson from our entire education system, which is held together because teachers get more than two weeks off a year. Teachers and students alike are mentally burnt to a crisp by the end of the school year. It's a long break that refreshes everyone and makes it possible to jump back into a new school year excited.

One last concern a friend recently shared with me was, *"So I definitely see the benefit to the workers, and maybe to the company, but what about the economy as a whole? Wouldn't this ruin the American economy?"* Now, I'm no economist, but if we add more jobs to cover that potential 8% reduction in work hours—lowering unemployment and giving people more free time to spend money—I don't know, but I think the economy will be just fine.

I've been able to take my kids to Disneyland in California a few times. As our only Disney experiences so far, it was incredible. But the week I write this, we are on an East Coast trip and staying at Disney World, Florida, for the first time. The California Disney seemed quite large, but driving into Disney World, it's enormous. Adam and I started talking about the kind of vision necessary to imagine this huge ecosystem before any of it existed. It's an incredible story that started in 1958 when Disney began researching new potential locations. In 1964, the company started buying up tracts of land with tremendous secrecy. In total, they were able to purchase over 27,000 acres for Disney World. Walt Disney was one of the greatest visionaries of the 20th century. It's hard to imagine a huge paradigm shift, like giving every employee a month off every year. But not everyone needs to see this vision. A few will see how all these benefits will give their company a huge advantage.

With enough demand from employees and a few visionary companies, we can change the way our working careers look. It's true that some companies would rather burn down than change.

CHAPTER TWELVE

Let them. When big trees burn, it creates space on the forest floor for diversity and new, stronger trees to rise up and take their place.

For more information on how you can support your employees to get the most benefit from their sabbatical, or for help creating or improving your sabbatical program, check out retireoften.com/book.

CHAPTER THIRTEEN

PACK YOUR MINI-RETIREMENT GO BAG

In my 20s, I was let go from a job. Kinda. Or I sort of quit. My position was being combined with another position which I was unqualified for and uninterested in. Either way, I was unexpectedly unemployed. It's a situation most people find themselves in at one point or another. And as usual, it was stressful and a bit sad. I was bumming around the house, applying for jobs, trying to get caught up on housework but generally feeling uninspired.

That could have been the whole story for me. Except this mini-retirement concept had been swirling around in my head for so long. So, instead of moping about week after week, I felt ready-ish to take action.

Since adopting our oldest son, Micah, from foster care, who was then 13, we had enjoyed a couple of adventures. A big Florida road trip with beaches and theme parks. Some camping in Shenandoah National Forest. Living in the D.C. area at the time, we hadn't made it to my home state of Montana and my favorite place growing up, Glacier National Park. Glacier had been magical for me as a child and I was desperate to share that with him.

Gaps in employment are a perfect opportunity for an impromptu mini-retirement. I felt the typical concerns, *"What if someone wants to interview me, and I'm gone?" "What if I miss out on a job?" "What if I spend this money, and then it takes forever to find a new job?"* But I was also prepared. We had paid off our debt by this point and were saving 50% of our income, which meant we could live on one income for a while.

The trip was everything I hoped for. We drove the Going-to-the

Sun Road, saw mountain goats, canoed on Lake McDonald, biked to Apgar Village and soaked in hot springs.

Looking back at all our mini-retirements, I don't regret any of them. In hindsight, all of them brought about pivotal growth: personally, in business, in passive income, and in relationships. But this one holds a special spot in my heart. Partly because it was the mini-retirement I was most scared to take. I had the most hesitation and excuses not to go, but that trip to Glacier National Park is a memory I can never replace.

HOW TO PACK

Life can present unexpected opportunities to take a step back from the 9–5 to focus on what matters to you. The key to grasping those opportunities is to be ready for them. Think about it like having a **go bag**.

If you have ever watched *NCIS*—or probably any crime drama—you might have noticed that the law enforcement agents always have a go bag. It's a small duffle bag that contains a few changes of clothes, toiletries, and anything else they might need for an unexpected trip. When they need to leave at a moment's notice, they grab the bag and are off to catch their flight.

When it comes to mini-retirements, there are a few things you can have ready so that you are ready to seize this opportunity at a moment's notice. I read an article about a married couple who were both laid off while one of them was still on maternity leave with their four-month-old baby. Undoubtedly, that adds to the stress and grief of losing a job. But knowing how magical a mini-retirement can be, a little part of me was excited for this couple. They will each receive four months of severance pay and six months of healthcare as part of the layoff. Having at least four months together with their newborn might be an incredible blessing when they look back

CHAPTER THIRTEEN

on it. If you're mentally, emotionally, and financially prepared, these hardships can be transformed into something beautiful. Here are ways you can prepare.

- **Cash.** Especially during a gap between jobs, you will want to have the money set aside beforehand. When you find an unplanned career break on your hands, it's hard to start saving to make this mini-retirement happen. Save up to cover your baseline expenses for time off, plus a little extra to go towards what you plan to do during your break.
- **Plans.** Finding yourself on an unexpected work break can be a little disorienting. It can be incredibly difficult to pivot from the discouragement, anger, and confusion of getting laid off. When you feel stuck in those emotions, it's hard to dream up and imagine an incredible adventure. It's helpful if you have done the process of imagining how you want to organize that mini-retirement before it happens. Note the mini-retirement adventures from Step One that would be perfect to do over a one-to-two-month time frame and on short notice. The more you have thought about what you want to do with this time, the more confident you'll feel embarking on this adventure.
- **Confidence.** Over the last 20 years, five of our dozen plus mini-retirements were unexpected. We didn't plan for a year in advance; instead, a life event happened (miscarriage, unemployment, mental health, and an adoption/rental purchase). These things are just part of life. They can be times of stress, uncertainty, and pain. But they can also be moments for joy, healing, and progress.

By having a plan and the savings to do it, you'll be halfway there. The other element is choosing to take action and lean into joy during hard times. Over time, mini-retirement after mini-retirement, you'll see how life-changing they are. You'll have confidence in the process.

YOU NEVER KNOW

I should have had a hundred opportunities to take my son, Micah, to Glacier National Park. Adam and I eventually moved to a town just outside the park. We would have gone into the park every holiday when he visited.

A few months after we moved back to Montana, Micah passed away without warning. That trip to Glacier was the only one we ever had together.

I had so many reasons not to take that trip. I stressed about it. I tried to talk myself out of it. I worried about taking a short break from work. All of those things I worried about, do you think I care one tiny bit about them now? No. A hundred times over, I would take that trip. Of all the family trips we had with Micah, that one was the most joyful. That's the trip we still talk about.

Life can be unpredictably fragile and short. You just never know. You never know if you'll have a hundred other chances to experience your dream, or if this is the last chance. Life changes, health changes, and circumstances change, frequently without any warning.

Save the money, make a plan, and when the opportunity arises, grab your go bag. And go.

STEP THREE

FIGURE OUT THE FINANCES

CHAPTER FOURTEEN

A MINI-RETIREMENT TO IMPROVE YOUR FINANCES

I KNOW A MINI-RETIREMENT can have a massive positive impact on your finances. I've seen it over and over again. The financial trajectory of my life and other people who have embarked on mini-retirements has improved. It seems a bit like magic. *"How does taking a career break improve your finances?"* The assumption is that a mini-retirement will put you back financially, not propel you forward. But there are six ways a mini-retirement can change your financial life.

SIX FINANCIAL PILLARS

I'm a money nerd—I always have been. I love numbers, spreadsheets, budgets, and financial projections. Those things have never created negative emotions for me, just joy. But I'm aware that's not the case for most people. For you, personal finance might be boring or terrifying; it isn't everyone's secret pleasure. Mini-retirement might be the carrot, and personal finance the stick. If so, mini-retirements are going to be amazing for your personal finances.

That's because it's the most painless way to master the six financial pillars essential to a life of freedom and flourishing. They are:

1. tracking your expenses
2. spending more intentionally
3. budgeting and creating financial plans
4. growing the gap (increase savings)
5. guarding the gap (investing and building new income)
6. financial empowerment.

In this step, you'll master all six of these financial pillars. If you have never done the first three, this mini-retirement is the perfect motivation. In chapter fifteen, you'll learn how to track your expenses and spend intentionally. In chapter sixteen, we will look at the budget for your mini-retirement adventure. And chapter seventeen will explore how growing the gap by 6.5%, through increasing income or reducing expenses, can unlock a lifetime of mini-retirements. Those first four pillars will fund your mini-retirement.

After your first mini-retirement, the next two pillars might surprise you. Something that could forever change your financial trajectory. First, after you experience the benefit of your sabbatical, you're ready to make bigger money moves because you are already dreaming up your next mini-retirement adventure. Many people start thinking more broadly about how to finance this with the fifth pillar, guarding the gap—increasing their income, adding new income, investing, starting a business or paying down debt. Once you start tasting an incredible lifestyle with seasons of work and seasons of leisure, there is a motivation to tackle larger financial goals.

The sixth pillar is financial empowerment as you put the first five pillars into action. Money stops being something that happens to you, all outside your control. You stop reacting to external forces. You realize that money can happen *for* you. You can create a plan, take steps, and make things happen. You're not playing defense, constantly adjusting to someone else's game. You're on offense; you have the strategy, and you are calling the plays. Your money doesn't control you, you control your money. As you master the tracking, budgeting, and saving, then start diversifying your income, you gain confidence.

CHAPTER FOURTEEN

A MINI-RETIREMENT BUDGET FOR EVERYONE

There is a nagging concern we need to talk about first. *"Can a person who makes as much as I do really afford a mini-retirement? Is it possible for **me**?"* I know it's a sticking point. People earning $25,000 a year have asked me. People earning $250,000 have asked me. Both have asked in all earnestness.

Are sabbaticals luxuries only the wealthy can afford? Or are they the benefit of having a low-paying but flexible job? I truly believe there is a mini-retirement for every budget, no matter your income. Regardless of what your financial journey looks like, you can enjoy a month-long mini-retirement with a bit of intention and planning. And after your first one you'll see how much more is possible. Even more controversial, everyone *deserves* at least one—one month in their life for rest, play, family, or personal growth.

I've lived two different financial lives. Growing up, there wasn't a lot to go around, and either through that situation or my natural personality, I became rather frugal. In our early 20s, Adam and I each earned about $30,000 a year and tried to live on half of that. The other half went to debt paydown; when our debts were cleared, we invested it.

In order to save half your income on modest salaries, you have to be very thoughtful about your spending. And you have to make some unconventional choices. When all our friends graduated with piles of student loan debt, Adam joined the military to help pay off that debt. When we were in our mid 20s in the D.C. area and starting to grow our family, we lived with a housemate to help cover our rent. During this season of life, we invested as much as we could and still took a half dozen mini-retirements. We opted for less expensive adventures, and for the most part we took turns, with one person staying employed.

In my 20s, a friend and I drove from D.C. to Seattle over the course of a month. We tent-camped in national and state parks. Stayed with family and slept on friends' couches. We filled thermoses with hot water when we stopped for gas to use for hot tea and instant oatmeal for breakfast. It was an incredible trip that I'm thankful I took. I'm also really glad I did it in my 20s because now, in my 40s, I no longer sleep on frozen ground. That season of my life has passed. In total, I spent about $1,500 on the month-long trip. When I look back at my 20s, it's still one of the highlights of that decade.

I've also lived a second financial life. When I was 32, we became financially independent. Our passive income from Adam's military pension, our rental properties, and our stock market investments covered all our bills and would indefinitely. We took a year off and then another year. Eventually, I started writing and coaching, and my business created some additional income. Over the last eight years, our investments have continued to grow, and our rental income has increased. We are no longer focused on accumulating more assets but instead on making sure our time is full of meaning and enjoyment. Our mini-retirements are now more often extended travel with our family. We have traded in our tent for a camper. Instead of gas station oatmeal, we splurge on trips to Disney. While it's probably more affordable than most might imagine, we definitely aren't optimizing for them to be super low-cost. We have the benefit of more passive income, more investments, and more cash flow.

Each season of life doesn't have to look the same. And I, for one, am going to enjoy the heck out of each decade of life and try to maximize the amount of time doing things that I'll look back on and say with a smile, *"Well, I'm glad I did it at that age because I'm never doing that stuff again!"*

CHAPTER FIFTEEN

FINDING YOUR BASELINE BUDGET

TWO OR THREE times a month for the last 20-some years, Adam and I have sat down to review our spending. I know this sounds like a nightmare scenario for some, because many conversations around money are filled with shame and conflict. Admittedly, the conversations were more tense at the beginning of our relationship. Now, it's a relaxing activity where we drink coffee, reflect, learn something new, get on the same page, and make small pivots. It's not exactly romantic, but it's definitely more fun than loading the dishwasher.

Tracking your monthly expenses is one of the most powerful tools to give you confidence when it comes time to step away from your 9–5. If your employer will be covering 100% of your pay while you're gone, you have more room to fudge this part. But if you need to save up to cover your living expenses, it helps to know what those are.

If you have very little idea where your money goes every month, it's very challenging to be confident that you've saved enough to cover your expenses during your mini-retirement. The clients that I see who have the most confidence in taking the leap are the ones who have been tracking their expenses for a long time. Ample savings helps, but knowing your numbers is a strong and simple first step.

A lot of people are resistant to the idea of budgeting. It feels restrictive and controlling, and to be honest, many feel like they're always failing. Budgeting can have its virtues, but that's not what's necessarily important to start. I suggest simply tracking. At the end of the month or the end of the year, you look to see where exactly your money went.

If you track your expenses for a few months, it's a great start and will provide a good snapshot of your monthly expenses. But I want you to consider the idea of finding a simple way for you to track your expenses long term—especially if you want to take longer mini-retirements, or if you are all in on the idea of retiring often being the rhythm of your working career. Having two or three years of detailed expenses can give you permission to take that leap.

OBSERVE + IMPROVE

When I'm working with clients who are trying to grow the gap between their income and their expenses, there are two elements of tracking that can be very useful: **observing** and **improving**.

The first step is to simply observe where your money went in a given month. It's an interesting phenomenon that a lot of people are hesitant even to observe their financial choices, as though not looking at them will mean that they didn't really happen. They fear they will feel regret or shame about the choices they made. The solution is to pretend it didn't happen and never look back. It can be easy to get stuck in the mindset of *"Let's not dwell on the past. Mistakes have been made, simply move forward and never speak of it again."* Obviously, this isn't the most productive way to engage with your finances. During observation, it's important to keep shame or judgment out of the process. This isn't an opportunity to belittle yourself or your partner. This is a time to be curious and open.

By observing the financial choices we make, it gives us an opportunity to see if that purchase lived up to expectations. Last month, you were doing the best you could with the information you had. Viewing this as an experiment in spending, having seen the outcomes, are there adjustments you might want to make going forward? What did you learn? How did spending that amount of money in that area feel? Is this spending a good reflection of your values and priorities?

The second step is to improve. You might think, *"Now is the point where I can beat myself up. I can feel guilty or start nagging my partner about all their bad choices."* Not so fast. After you have observed where your money went and what it was spent on, now is the opportunity to consider a question. Knowing what I know now, would I do anything different in the future? You don't look at past choices with shame, regret, or anger. All those choices are finished and can't be redone. Instead, you look for insight and understanding. These choices might present themselves again in the future. Knowing what you know now, do you want to handle it the exact same way? Having seen the outcome of your choices, would you want to adjust your choices in the future slightly?

When I started working with Rebecca, she and her partner had a very high income, but were struggling to make ends meet. They had a fair amount of debt and not much in the way of savings. Rebecca was very burned out at her job and was desperate for a career break ASAP. We started with simple purchase tracking and observation. One of the expenses that stuck out to them was that they were averaging about $700 a month towards alcohol purchases.

They said they enjoyed a couple of nice bottles of wine at home during the month, and when they went out to eat a couple of times a week, they often added an $80 bottle of wine to their dinner. Before tracking, it hadn't seemed like a big or significant expense. They weren't drinking excessively by any means, just a couple of glasses of wine here and there.

This could be an expense that they could have felt judgmental towards themselves about, but instead, I wanted to take a non-pejorative viewpoint. In light of their financial and long-term goals, was this expense adding as much enjoyment or relaxation as they anticipated it would? Was there perhaps a different way to allocate that $700 that could bring them closer to their goal and still provide some enjoyment and relaxation throughout their month? We weren't looking to change the past or to put a lot of labels or blame on past choices. Instead, the goal was to reflect on the value that they had received from those purchases and decide if they wanted to make any adjustments going into the next month based on their reflections.

HIGH VALUE/LOW VALUE

Simply lowering your spending month after month isn't always the goal. Instead, improving your spending may mean adjusting how you allocate your money to bring you more fun, relaxation, or meaning.

For example, maybe you're spending a fair amount on takeout food, but it would actually be more meaningful to invite friends over for a dinner party. You could shift some of that money from takeout food to buy the extra ingredients and food to host those dinner parties. In your observation, you'll realize that a few of your expenses were incredibly high value, and it gives you the information to know to include more of those types of expenses in the future. Tracking isn't always about spending less, but instead spending in more meaningful ways as you make progress to prepare for your mini-retirement.

There will be other expenses that provide less value than you anticipated. Now you have the information to reduce or eliminate those expenses and allocate money towards another area that you think could provide the value that you're hoping for. For example, you may have an expensive car payment with the hopes that driving a nicer car will make the commute to work more bearable and balance out some of the stress of your job. But after a while, you've adapted to this nicer car, and you don't really notice the features or the comfort. If you were to trade it in for a more affordable car and allocate that money towards a housekeeper so that when you come home, your house is more organized and tidy and you have more free time for hobbies, how would that impact your life? You might realize that this switch gets you closer to a more meaningful outcome. These realizations are more likely to happen when you set aside time each month to observe your financial choices and think about ways to improve them going forward.

The purpose of your mini-retirement is to have time for areas of your life that matter to you. The practice of tracking your expenses and better allocating money to the areas that matter will be the training wheels of your retire often lifestyle. If you have a partner that you share your financial life with, you have the perfect practice ground for intentional living conversations.

QUICK AND DIRTY CALCULATION

When I'm trying to help people calculate their monthly expenses, and they've never tracked a day in their life, there is a quick and dirty method they can use. This won't give you as much helpful information, and it's not 100% accurate, but it will give you a ballpark idea of where you're starting from.

The first step is to figure out what your take-home pay is from all sources of employment or income. If you're self-employed, you should look at past tax returns to figure out what your after-tax income is. Then, from this take-home pay, you deduct any retirement investing or savings that you made that year. You can also deduct large one-time expenses that won't happen again, such as a down payment for a house. Once you subtract these from your take-home pay, the amount left is about what you spent that year or that month.

So, if your combined take-home pay is $100,000 that year, you put $15,000 into retirement accounts and $10,000 into your kids' 529 accounts, you probably spend about $75,000 on your living expenses. That means your monthly expenses are about $6,250. With this number, you can add back the amount that you spent on healthcare and insurance.

If you've never tracked any of your expenses, this will at least give you a starting point to help figure out what your mini-retirement budget should be. Over the next few months or years, if you start tracking your expenses, you can adjust your numbers with more accurate information.

EXPENSES GO UP

After you have an idea of your baseline budget, you can start adjusting that number for your mini-retirement. There will be some expenses that will go up once you separate from an employer. The biggest of these, depending on where you live, is likely your healthcare. But there might be other benefits that your employer provides, and when you separate you will have to cover those costs. So as you're figuring out your baseline budget, take that starting number and add in these new or extra expenses.

EXPENSES GO DOWN

There will also be some expenses that, if you are no longer employed, will go down. The cost of commuting, professional attire, or workplace lunches go down. For some people, their costs naturally drop a few hundred dollars a month when they're no longer working. They're ordering less takeout, cooking at home more, and simply paying for fewer time-saving conveniences. Particularly in

America, being short on time tends to be expensive. Once you have more time, things become more affordable.

Another huge factor in your costs going down, especially if you plan to be traveling during your mini-retirement, is housing. Sometimes, people plan mini-retirements during natural relocation points in their careers. Melissa and her family planned a mini-retirement when she and her husband separated from their jobs. They moved out of their California home, saving that rent cost, while traveling through Central America. After their mini-retirement they relocated to Michigan. They did store their furniture, which was a small additional cost, but not having to pay rent dramatically reduced the amount of income they needed for their mini-retirement.

Your formula for calculating your baseline mini-retirement budget is your current expenses plus whatever new expenses you might incur minus the expenses that will go down once you're no longer employed. You can take this baseline number and multiply it by the number of months you're planning on a mini-retirement. For example, if your baseline number is $4,000 and you're planning on taking a three-month mini-retirement, the baseline number you'll need is $12,000.

This first step of tracking your monthly expenses is a huge advantage for taking mini-retirements. It's worth the time and effort to set up a weekly or monthly time to have a **money date**. Spend some time with your money, be curious, open and non-judgmental. Make observations about the value you received from your purchases, then be creative on how you can improve making next month even better.

Now that you know your baseline budget for your regular expenses, let's look at how much money you'll need to pay for the adventures you have planned during your mini-retirement.

CHAPTER SIXTEEN

BUILD YOUR DREAM BUDGET

I'VE HAD A job that filled me with dread. Sinking feelings would begin on Sunday nights. Then, Monday morning, I would sit in my car in the parking lot and try to take slow deep breaths to hedge off the panic. If you have ever felt stuck in a place you don't want to be, you know there isn't much that alleviates that weight. One small solace was when I would mentally escape into my Google spreadsheet. I had been dreaming of a big U.S. road trip with our kids while they were still young enough to think it was cool. Occasionally, during a break, I would pull up my à la carte road trip budget. That dream budget helped me get through the last few months before I made the leap into my mini-retirement. The dream started feeling real once I had the plan and the budget.

There are two elements to your mini-retirement budget. Your baseline expenses, which you discover through tracking, and the **dream budget**. Your dream budget is the extra cost for the things you will be doing on your mini-retirement. If you are planning on spending your time doing local hikes and gardening, your cost might be almost insignificant. On the other hand, if you are planning an around-the-world trip for your family, you might need an extra $80,000. Your dream budget takes all those plans and puts a specific cost to your dream.

HOW TO CREATE AN
À LA CARTE PRICE LIST

The best way to build your dream budget is by creating an à la carte price list.

On a breakfast menu, you have meals listed, like the Big Breakfast Special: two eggs with two slices of toast, two pieces of bacon, and hash browns. But you can also order à la carte. This is how I almost always order breakfast because I don't eat eggs, and every darn meal comes with eggs. A side of hash browns. A side of ham. A side with one biscuit and gravy.

Same thing with travel or large experiences, like hiking for three months in Europe. You can think about three months in Europe as a $15,000 experience. Or you can break down the price with an à la carte dream price list. You list the costs for flights, hotels in different countries, activities, food, and transportation. Not only will it help you plan better and create a more accurate budget, but you will find loads of motivation knowing each small step you make is tangible progress towards your dream.

CREATING THE À LA CARTE
PRICE LIST

Plan: First, you need to pin down what exactly you want to do. When you do your research, you can add line items for each expense. As you add more details to your plan, you can modify the budget items. But you need to start with a basic plan. I started putting together my U.S. road trip price list with all the elements of our trip I could think of: campsites, gas per 1,000 miles, and excursions we might enjoy.

CHAPTER SIXTEEN

DREAM PRICE LIST EXAMPLE

Mini-Retirement Expense	Expected	Amount
Accommodations		
1 night of camping (state/national park)	$15	
1 night of camping (simple campground)	$30	
1 night of camping (deluxe campground)	$50	
1 month of camping (15 state parks, 10 simple, 5 deluxe)	**$775**	
Entertainment		
1 year of National Park Pass	$80	
1 year of Science Museum Family Pass	$70	
1 fun activity ($7 per person x 7 people)	$49	
1 treat (i.e. ice cream) $3 per person x 7	$21	
Monthly fun budget (park & museum pass, +2 fun activities/month & 1 treat/wk)	**$184**	
Gas Cost		
1,000 miles (20mpg @ $3 a gallon)	$150	
2,000 miles (20mpg @ $3 a gallon)	$300	
Misc. Cost		
Tank of propane	$8	
Load of laundry	$3	
Day at a theme park	$300	
McDonald's stop	$15	
TOTAL AMOUNT BUDGETED:	**$1,585**	
TOTAL AMOUNT SAVED:		
DIFFERENCE:		

Research: Start researching each individual cost of your trip or experience. This is something you can do while you watch TV at night. Or are on a break at work. I started a Google sheet and would just add elements and notes as I found the price options. You can compile your list over the course of six months—places you would want to see or stay. Routes you might want to take. You might find out you can get a one-way flight from Rome to Barcelona for under $100. Or that there are great campsites with cabins in Croatia for under $50 a night. When I took a summer to create a food forest, I initially thought I would spend $8,000. As I started to add line items and allowed some project creep, the total cost came to $12,000… for the first year. Expansions have been made every summer since. Your dream budget might show that your adventure is more affordable than you imagined. Or, in the case of a flagstone patio, a little more expensive.

Start "buying" items: I set up a separate checking account named "dream fund." As I was able to save $100 or $1,000, I knew exactly what that amount of cash would pay for. It wasn't just $100 towards a $15,000 goal, but each amount I saved served a specific part of my budget. Having a budget broken down into specific items provides four important benefits.

1. Motivation

When you have a dream that is incredibly important to you, and you can see how your actions get you closer to that dream, it makes motivation easy. In a way, you are just choosing between two things you want to buy. You can have that takeout lunch now for $12 or use that money to buy the parking pass to see Mount Rushmore. You aren't just "saving"; you are "buying" items to fulfill your dream. You won't pay for them now, but you are buying them mentally. Instead of ordering a pizza this weekend, you stash that money away to buy a pizza in Rome.

This motivation also applies to earning extra income. Your side hustle earned you $900, which will cover a month in a resort in the Philippines. It can also provide motivation to make some changes to your current expenses. You switch your cell phone plan and, each month, that saving pays for another fun travel experience. The first month it paid for your admission into the Louvre. The next month it buys your admission to the Anne Frank house. In the third month, the saving may be enough to take in *Phantom of the Opera* in London.

2. New opportunities

Knowing exactly what you need, you see new ways to go about getting that. You find a credit card rewards program that will give you great travel miles. You start talking to people who have done something similar, and you find out about an amazing museum pass for $70. You start noticing the right time of year to find good deals on campers. You sign up for the travel emails and see what kinds of deals you can piece together.

3. Support

It's hard for your friends and family to tangibly support a vague goal like, *"I would like to travel someday."* But if they know exactly what you need, those become awesome birthday and Christmas gifts. From buying travel books, donating some airline miles, or gift cards to restaurants you can use on your trip. If you have kids, you can buy things they would like for the trip as holiday gifts. Giving $50 towards a $30,000 travel fund goal might not seem meaningful, but maybe your mom would love to buy a new travel suitcase for your trip as a holiday gift.

4. Preparation

The sooner you flesh out what you want to do, the better you can prepare. Because we had been planning a big U.S. road trip for five years, we had time to test out a few details. We bought a pop-up camper and did a six-week trip one summer. We did a two-week trip the following summer, which gave me a better idea of all of the costs of traveling. We learned how we like to travel (how many miles on drive days, how long we stay places, how many activities to fit into a week). I had time to get to know other people who travel with kids. We had a better idea of whether we wanted to travel in a pop-up or buy a hard-sided camper. We realized that we could rent out our house for about the same amount as it would cost us to travel full time.

Until I started writing out my à la carte dream price list, I had no idea how much something like this would cost, how to get started, or ways to test and learn about it. It was just a big dream that felt a bit impossible. Once you have your baseline cost and your dream budget, your next step is finding ways to fund your mini-retirement.

CHAPTER SEVENTEEN

6.5% FOR A LIFETIME OF MINI-RETIREMENTS

A MAGICAL BASELINE

IN THIS CHAPTER I want to show you how saving an additional 6.5% gives you access to a lifetime full of mini-retirements. With it you can accomplish a whole bucket list of dreams and goals.

To start, I'd like to paint a picture of what it might look like to take a month off every other year. Imagine you start at 22, with plans to permanently retire at 68.

24 years old: Teaching English in Korea
26 years old: Volunteering on farm in Hawaii
28 years old: Silent retreat
30 years old: Road trip with family
32 years old: Camping in national parks
34 years old: Biking through France with brother
36 years old: Learning Spanish in Mexico with family
38 years old: Hiking Camino
40 years old: Renting lake house with family
42 years old: Building Habitat for Humanity house
44 years old: Disney trip
46 years old: European vacation with spouse and teenagers
48 years old: Writing the first draft of a book
50 years old: Helping mom with her garden
52 years old: Spanish courses in Costa Rica and surfing

54 years old: Cooking classes in Italy

56 years old: Learning to watercolor paint

58 years old: Yoga retreat in Thailand with friends

60 years old: Back to theme parks with grandkids

62 years old: Biking through Croatia

64 years old: Mediterranean cruise

6.5%

Imagine you have 20 incredible experiences like this on your bucket list and are ready to start crossing them off. Here is the math of how you can take one month off every other year for the rest of your career.

In the previous chapters you figured out your baseline budget, how much your normal life costs. In this scenario, you'll have to cover that expense. Now, if your employer gives you the month off paid, all the better! You can save a smaller percentage or have extra money to take a more luxurious trip. But for this example, we'll assume your time off is unpaid. We will also assume that you are spending pretty much all the money you're making. So to cover a month's expenses you need to save 4.5% of your income for 24 months.

Monthly expenses math

For every $1,000 of monthly take-home pay, saving 4.5% is $45.

Save that monthly $45 for 24 months (two years) and you have $1,080. Which is only slightly higher than the $1,000 of take-home pay.

Of course, this scales to however much your take-home pay is, because the percentage is the same. For example: $5,000 × 4.5% = $225. $225 × 24 months = $5,400, which is just slightly more than your take-home pay.

So to replace a month's take-home pay, you need to save 4.5%.

Dream budget math

A good rule of thumb across all the mini-retirement plans I've reviewed is that a mini-retirement averages about an additional 50% of people's average month expenses.

In the dream budget chapter, you should have worked out exactly how much this adventure will cost. But, for this example, we aren't just thinking about one specific next mini-retirement but this idea of a lifetime of one-month mini-retirements, with the cost of each varying. So if you typically spend $5,000 a month to live, the average cost for your month-long mini-retirement will be an extra $2,500 on top of the $5,000, or $7,500 total. If you typically spend $10,000 a month, your mini-retirement will average an additional $5,000 per month or $15,000 total.

Fifty percent is a rather generous assumption. I've seen many people spend only their typical monthly budget while on sabbatical. If they spend $60,000 a year on normal life, they can travel around the world for $60,000. And many people spend even less. I interviewed a couple on my podcast who moved their family to France for two years. They spent about $40,000 a year in France, which was the same as their childcare costs back home! Being on sabbatical was massively cheaper than their normal life. Nevertheless, let's assume 50%. That means you'll need to save another 2% for the sabbatical cost.

For every $1,000 of take-home pay, 2% is $20. $20 × 24 months = $480. Now that is slightly below 50% of the $1,000, but remember from above the 4.5% was slightly higher. Again, the math scales no matter what your take-home pay is. For example, if your take-home pay is $5,000, $5,000 × 2% = $100, and $100 × 24 months = $2,400.

So 6.5% will give you enough to replace your normal take-home pay plus an extra 50% for your dream budget. For each $1,000 of take-home pay, you save 6.5% = $65 × 24 months = $1,560.

Saving 4.5% for living cost + 2% for sabbatical costs = saving an extra 6.5% of your income to afford a month off every two years for life.

In the table here we have three scenarios. One of them might be similar to your salary now.

DREAM BUDGET MATH

	Person A	Person B	Person C
Monthly take-home Pay	$3,000	$5,000	$10,000
Baseline Budget	$3,000	$5,000	$10,000
Dream Budget	$1,500	$2,500	$5,000
Monthly Contribution	$200	$325	$650

With these three scenarios, I want to explore what it would look like to grow the gap by increasing income or reduce expenses to save the additional 6.5% that will fund all your adventures.

GROW THE GAP, GUARD THE GAP

If I had to predict someone's financial success based on their ability to implement one idea, it would be this concept: **grow the gap, guard the gap**. Growing the gap means increasing the amount of

CHAPTER SEVENTEEN

money between your income and your expenses. People do that by some combination of increasing income or reducing expenses. Guarding the gap means using that extra cash flow in ways that are productive towards your long-term financial goals.

In an upcoming chapter, I'll show you how to use the five buckets to be able to afford longer and more luxurious mini-retirements by being strategic with "guarding the gap." But in this chapter, I want you to see that you can "grow the gap" by thoughtfully reducing a few expenses, and find ways to increase your income a bit.

Increase income

There are two categories of increased income: increasing your primary income or adding/increasing secondary income. For people with high-earning career fields, increasing their primary income might be a strong lever. In one to two years, you might be able to get a raise or promotion that would cover the entire 6.5%, with no need to reduce any expenses or add any new income. If you make $10,000 a month (person C), that is a $7,800 yearly raise. If you set aside just one of your 6.5% raises, even if you spent all future raises, you could fund all your mini-retirements. A 6.5% raise would be below what is typically achieved by switching jobs. If you can't negotiate the month off, you could find a new job with that raise and take a month off in between jobs by pushing back your start date. Often, the people with the highest salaries also have the largest time commitments to their work. So, earning more at their primary job is the best way to increase their income.

For some careers, there aren't many promotion options, and even 3% raises are hard to come by. Thankfully, there are lots of other ways to increase your income. Side hustles, part-time jobs, or real estate. The $200–$300 monthly savings could easily be accomplished with low-barrier tasks like childcare or yard work.

I know a lot of people who make $200 a month pet sitting. There is a misconception that mini-retirements aren't accessible to low earners. Part-time housekeepers earn $50 an hour in my area. With six hours a month at $50 an hour that would allow you to save an extra $300 a month, enough for a life filled with mini-retirements. If you are a high earner, you might be able to do some consulting in your professional field. Another possibility is taking a job that aligns with your mini-retirement. One year, Adam, who loves to ski, worked as seasonal help at a sporting goods store. He was able to get a free ski pass and a good discount on new skis. I have a social worker friend who loves to travel, and for over a decade she has worked part time at the airport. The shifts fit around her day job, and she and her family can fly free or very cheap. I took mini-retirements as a low earner, and saving an extra 6.5% might only be $200–$300 a month. Also low-income jobs tend to be easier to replace if you need to separate from your employer.

Growing the gap is helpful no matter what path you take: excel at your job to get a raise or promotion, find a better paying job, take on a side job or side hustle. But if that's not possible or appealing, you can always focus on the other side of the coin, reducing expenses.

Reduce expenses

Transportation, housing, and food are most people's three biggest expenses. Reduce any of those by $300 a month, and your mini-retirement could be paid for. Or work towards reducing all of them by $100 a month. When I was learning to cook, I focused on food items that cost less than $1 a pound: carrots, potatoes, onions, apples, bananas, pasta, rice, beans, etc. If those types of ingredients made up 80% of my recipes, the grocery bill was naturally lower. Over the years, I found recipes that were easy, tasty, nutritious, and also happened to be affordable. For over a decade, we aimed to save

50% of our income, and our income wasn't huge, so I experimented with all types of frugality.

There are countless ways to reduce your spending. Start with one low-effort, high-return thing. Even if you only make one small change a month, it won't take long to create that 6.5% savings rate.

Remember, it's not about deprivation. You're not skipping out on eating out, you're just saving it for your next trip. Instead of the generic chain burritos, you'll be eating street tacos in Mexico. You aren't setting this money aside so you hopefully can retire in 30 years, you're just delaying the enjoyment until your next incredible mini-retirement in one to two years.

FIVE PRINCIPLES FOR GROWING THE GAP

For those who really struggle imagining how to grow the gap, here are five principles that will make your efforts much more effective with less stress.

1. Not all advice is applicable

In my early 20s, I had a friend who bemoaned the fact that all the articles online about ways to save money weren't applicable to her. She wasn't able to reduce her daily coffee budget because she never bought coffee out. She couldn't get rid of a gym membership that she never had. In reality, she was already incredibly frugal and implementing almost every money-saving technique out there. When it comes to reducing your expenses, you can only go so far down. At some point, your expenses will be fully optimized. In order to grow her gap, it was time to start focusing on the other side of the equation: increasing income.

For reasons a psychologist could probably explain, there is a tendency to focus on the advice that won't work. I've seen people use it to help justify why they feel stuck. Not all advice will be applicable. It's fine to acknowledge that, or even be bummed by it. But don't focus on what won't work for you. There are a number of levers you can pull to grow your gap. We all have different challenges and different opportunities.

2. Start with low effort and high impact

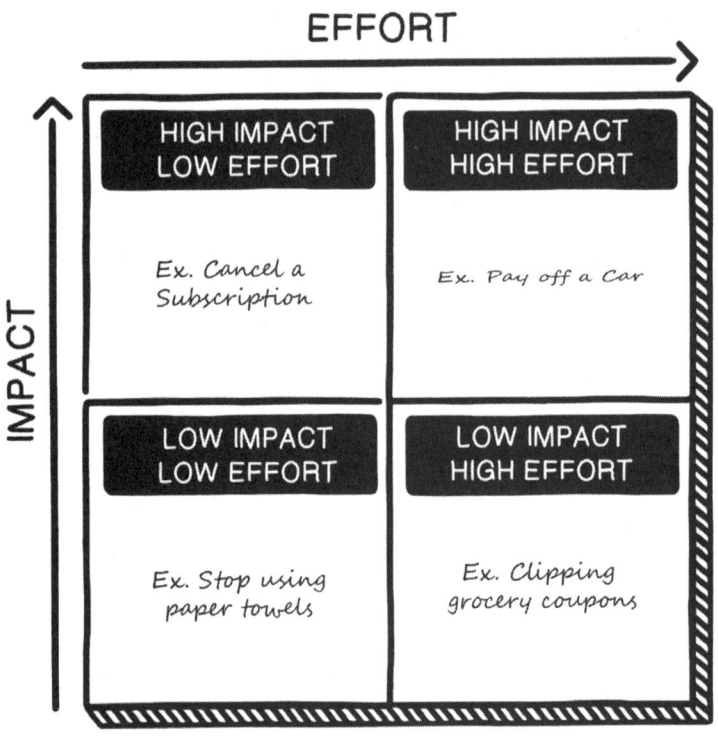

There are things that will take more effort and things that will take less effort. Some actions will make a big impact, some will make a small impact. If you have to start somewhere, pick the things that require little effort and have a high impact. Maybe you can cancel subscriptions you aren't using. It will take 30 minutes, one time, and save you $75 a month ongoing.

3. One thing at a time

It's easy to be overwhelmed when going into "money-saving mode." Pick one thing. Make one change. Maybe that's one change a week, or one change a month. You don't need to reinvent your life on day one. Thoughtful consistency with your money will serve you better than a scorched-earth plan you can't maintain for more than a month.

4. Gain momentum for bigger changes

Because you started with easy and high-reward changes, you have some really exciting momentum. It hasn't been hard, but you are seeing real progress! You can start to leverage that momentum and excitement into bigger and more challenging changes. One guest on my podcast had an amazing first mini-retirement. By the time she and her spouse returned home, they both knew this wouldn't be a one-time thing. They wanted to do this every year for the rest of their lives. They took a big step, hired a contractor, and created a small apartment in their large home. That extra income alone would fully fund their yearly adventures.

5. 30% different

I've seen so many people stuck in financial discouragement. Things are already so hard, and change feels out of reach. If you can't imagine change for yourself, look to how others are doing it. I frequently hear, *"There is no way to live on less than my salary in my area!"* But if you look carefully, I bet there are people in your community who make 30% less than you. How do they do it? How do they make it work? Not that you have to do all those things, but their life can give some concrete examples of how it's done.

Of course, you absolutely don't have to reduce your expenses. You could opt to increase your income. Here, again, look at people with similar education or in your field who make 30% more than you. How did they do it? Did they go back to school, take extra classes, switch fields, switch companies, or network? Again, you don't have to do any of those things. However, there is a road map that could provide some specific inspiration and direction if you look around for examples of people who are doing it.

A lifetime filled with mini-retirements isn't a pipe dream. Grow the gap by an additional 6.5% and you can unlock it. You don't have to do anything drastic because there are literally a thousand different ways to go about it. Any combination of increasing income and/or reducing your expenses by 6.5%, and the bucket list of experiences is yours for the taking.

CHAPTER EIGHTEEN
OLD AGE AND IN BETWEEN

IMAGINE HAVING $5M in retirement accounts and feeling like you have no options to take a break from work, even for a year, let alone retire early. For those with 20 bucks in their checking account, it seems like a bizarre, rich-person problem. And it is, I suppose.

As I chatted on a Zoom call with Mindy, this was a problem nonetheless. Her and her husband's story was familiar. They had gotten serious about investing in their 20s and started maxing out their retirement accounts. Soon they were also investing significant amounts of money in a brokerage account. They both made a great income and, other than their mortgage payment, didn't spend excessively. Basically, they thought they had done everything right. Now in their 40s, compound interest combined with consistent investing meant their net worth was in the millions.

And yet, they felt stuck. They wanted a change, and that's why they signed up for coaching. But they didn't feel like they had many options. They weren't sure they had enough to retire forever. They were nervous they wouldn't be able to find good-paying jobs again like the ones they were considering leaving. It's not that they hated their jobs, except they were tired. Tired of the commuting, the long hours, the stress, and the monotony of it.

They had two small kids and just wanted more time as a family. Maybe even rekindle old hobbies or start volunteering. Their marriage was fine, but they didn't feel like newlyweds anymore between work and kids. Most of their conversations felt like business partners managing day-to-day life. How did they do everything right, and still end up feeling like they didn't have any freedom to do the things they wanted or needed? I've had this exact same conversation a hundred times with a hundred people. Your money can give you security. Your money can give you freedom. **Very few people figure out how their money can give them both security and freedom.** But your money *can* give you both. Let me show you how.

SECURITY + FREEDOM

People seem to gravitate towards security *or* freedom. Maybe because of personality or upbringing, one of the two often seems particularly desirable and worth pursuing. But you don't have to choose. Both are possible.

Allowing your money to give you security means you can handle an unexpected layoff. When an emergency happens, you have the funds to ease the pain. Security means you'll have enough money, when you can no longer work, to cover your expenses. These are all great things. Despite popular online notions, your 401(k) is not a scam! Retirement investment accounts are amazing tools to grow your wealth and provide income in retirement.

Your money can also give you freedom. It can give you options and choices. Freedom means you can leave a bad situation. Freedom means you can take unexpected opportunities. You are able to honor your needs and chase your dreams. This freedom allows you to lean into those seasons of life with expiration dates. You have the agency to design a life that reflects your values and goals.

When I was about 12, I begged my mom to leave her marriage. Life in the home didn't feel safe or good. I didn't care about the cost or logistics, I just wanted us to get out. She very practically and honestly said she couldn't afford to raise three kids on her own. I went upstairs to my room and cried hot tears into my pillow. I was devastated, angry, and scared. But I also had an epiphany. Money gives you choices. It gives you options. At that moment, I knew I wanted more options. And I never wanted to feel stuck this way again. So, as soon as I could work, I got a job and started saving, $20 and $100 at a time. I wanted security, and I wanted freedom. Money was how I was going to get both.

WANT BOTH

There are books about securing your retirement and making sure you don't eat dog food as an elderly person. There are books on how life is short, and YOLO. Those simple, extreme narratives often win. But I think you should want both. Security *and* freedom. Because people who only have one might say they are happy, but there is an undercurrent of fear. If you always live for the moment, those feelings of dread still creep in. *"Will I have enough to ever retire? What if I lose my job? What if I end up in poverty at 70?"* As much as they enjoy the present, the future carries some fear.

People who optimize for security might feel smug because they never have those fears. They know they will be taken care of in old age. But there is another fear. *"Am I missing out on time with my kids? What if I never tried out that business idea or pursued my dream? What if I look back with regrets? Am I wasting my best years?"*

The extreme of freedom or security isn't serving you. There is magic in the middle. Freedom and security. And people do it. They have fully funded retirement accounts and take around-the-world trips. They aren't stressed about the future, and are taking frequent mini-retirements to enjoy the present. These people don't need to earn hundreds of thousands of dollars a year or be born with a trust fund. This is possible for normal people.

TWO IMPORTANT BARRELS

If you want to create a financial life that has abundant freedom and security, there are two buckets you want to fill: an **old age** bucket and an **in-between** bucket.

Your old age barrel

Your old age barrel will give you money when you are no longer able to work. Think of it like traditional retirement savings. With this barrel, there are a few rules. The biggest rule is don't let it run out! When you are in your traditional retirement, it's important that the barrel never runs dry. Most financial planners subscribe to the "4% rule." The 4% rule is based on research that you can pull 4% of your investments every year, adjusting the number up to match inflation, for 30 years and have a good chance of your money never running out. For example, if you have $1m invested, 4% is $40,000 a year you could spend. Of course, some people prefer 3% or 5% or 6%. Everyone has their own formula, but we all agree that the plan is for your assets to never get to zero while you're still alive and needing that income.

Your in-between barrel

I 100% believe you should put some money in that old age barrel. But I think you should also have a second barrel, an in-between barrel. The in-between barrel is money you can use at will between now and old age. It's a slush fund. It's a YOLO fund. It's "No, thank you" (or FU) money. It's an opportunity fund or an "oh crap" fund.

Your in-between fund will pay for your mini-retirements. It will help you stay home with kids for a few years. It will let you start a business or write a book or build a tiny house. The difference between your old age fund and your in-between fund is that the in-between fund has no rules. It's not supposed to last indefinitely. It should run out. Use it however you like. It's like a college fund; it was set aside for a purpose, but it only fulfills that purpose if you use it. No one creates a college fund that will pay out 4% for school forever. Use it up! For example, if you had $50,000 in your in-between fund, you could use 100% on a year off, fill it back up over a couple of years, use $10,000 to start a business, fill it up, use $25,000 for another mini-retirement, refill, use $10,000 on a classic car, take another mini-retirement… whatever you want!

Your in-between barrel gives you freedom and security. If someone totals your car, you can use it to buy a new car. You are in a job you hate, quit. Take a mini-retirement then find a new job. It allows you to get yourself out of a bad spot and seize opportunities when they arrive.

Yes, save for old age! Don't live with the low-level dread that poverty might be awaiting you once you can no longer work. *And* save for the in between. Don't fear that you are missing out on the most beautiful and exciting parts of life. Want both. Pursue both. The real magic is when you create both.

How much you save for old age retirement will depend on how you want to fill the five buckets, which is our next chapter. For the old age barrel, you can simply put 10–20% into a retirement account, but there are a variety of options for how people create income for their old age.

CHAPTER NINETEEN
FILL THE FIVE BUCKETS

A FTER COLLEGE, MY friend Chad wasn't sure what he wanted to do professionally. He didn't love the idea of a 9–5 corporate job. But like a lot of 22-year-olds, he lacked the skills, knowledge, and resources to build his own company. Not that he wasn't a smart and capable guy. He had played college football and gotten good grades. But like many college graduates realize, being good at college doesn't make success automatic after you accept your diploma. So he took what he had: hard work and a willingness to learn and tried to get into real estate. He started with little money but a big pile of optimism and hustle.

Chad was like a lot of people in their 20s that I met. Still hopeful that maybe they could have purpose in their work, make a difference, build wealth, and pursue their adventures and dreams. Chad wanted both. Freedom and security.

In this chapter, I want to show you how some additional options are unlocked by "guarding the gap." Of course, you can just save your additional gap—that 6.5%—in a bank account, and enjoy your mini-retirements. No fuss. But if you are hoping for longer or more extravagant mini-retirements, you can also be strategic about diversifying your investment and income with the five buckets. These five buckets will help fill up your old age barrel and in-between barrel.

Chad and I are both in our 40s now. He's taken multiple mini-retirements. He has built out four of five buckets over the last 20 years. He invests in the stock market (bucket #1), keeps enough cash (bucket #2), built a business (bucket #4), and he and his business partner own 100 rentals (bucket #5), along with other passive income. His income and investments are diversified. Like we talked about in the last chapter, he has freedom and security.

So many people are resigned to work forever and die broke. The important takeaway from Chad's story is that it wasn't quick or easy. But it's also possible. You need to have a different mindset and take a slightly different path. If you like the idea of retiring often, consider moving in the direction of building and filling the five buckets. This is the second half of grow the gap, guard the gap. The five buckets are where you guard the gap you've grown. And in time, the five buckets will help you grow the gap even more.

FINDING THE FIVE BUCKETS

The five buckets are the five types of assets that create the most financial freedom, security, and flexibility. The stock market, cash, hourly work, building a business, rentals and house hacking—and a bonus bucket of debt paydown. These are the buckets where you can put the gap you have grown. In time, these buckets will also create cash flow or income for you. This is how the rich get richer. Their money starts making money.

Before you get overwhelmed, just know you don't *have* to do any of this. All of this is optional. Just like I said two chapters ago, you can save a couple hundred dollars a month, shove it under your mattress, and take a mini-retirement every other year. But if something about the idea of freedom and security resonates with you, if you dream of longer and more extravagant mini-retirements, if you want a good-sized pile of old age money and in-between money, the five buckets are how you fill up those two barrels. Just like growing the gap, focus on the areas you have the most opportunity in and skim past the ones that won't work. You don't need all five. Start with one, and build as you go.

CHAPTER NINETEEN

Bucket 1. The stock market

There are two main ways to invest in the stock market. There are tax-advantaged retirement accounts, like a 401(k) or IRA in the U.S. (most countries have equivalents). With each type of account, there are rules on how you can put money in and take money out. A quick Google search can explain those rules, or there are a hundred great books on how those types of accounts work. The second option is a brokerage account. It functions like a savings account, except it holds stocks and bonds instead of just cash. Like a savings account, you can put in and take out however much you want, whenever you want. Both retirement accounts and brokerage accounts are powerful and helpful.

Unfortunately, most people only add money to their retirement accounts. While I never want to discourage people from filling up their retirement accounts, only funding those accounts doesn't lend itself to a life full of mini-retirements and options. They were designed for the "work 40 years and then retire until you die" model of our parents' and grandparents' generations.

While there are technical workarounds to allow you to pull money out before retirement age, here's the dirty little secret no one wants to talk about. Pulling money out of your retirement accounts early isn't as technically hard as it is emotionally and psychologically tough. It just feels *wrong*. People have dutifully tucked money away for retirement, and to sneak some out of the account to take a round-the-world trip, write a book or start a business feels like you're breaking open your piggy bank before it's full. You worked so hard to get that money in there! Now to rob the account early, for such a frivolous luxury, is a tough mental barrier to jump.

Retirement accounts are a wonderful place to store and grow your old age money. And they can be good tools for mini-retirements if you are clear about that intention. But a brokerage account is ideal when it comes to investing in the stock market to help fund your in-between money barrel.

Bucket 2. Cash

Cash is perhaps the most underrated asset. Maybe because it doesn't grow and compound like stocks or real estate. But what it lacks in growth it makes up for in freedom. Cash gives people the confidence to make a change in their lives.

When the 4% rule looks at your investment accounts, it tells you no to your dreams. You could have a million invested in retirement accounts, and based on the 4% rule, your money could still veto your mini-retirement. The cash account says YES! Cash is one of the simplest to set up and easiest buckets to fill. Any checking or savings account will work. Earn an extra $20 and throw it in there.

Cash also gives you the best short-term bang for your buck. If your mini-retirement is going to cost $15,000 and you have $15,000 in cash, you can use 100% of that and you're done. Versus things like real estate, where you might have $100,000 equity in a property that earns you $10,000 a year in rental profit. That might have taken a few years to even get the cash flow to this point. Cash is a one-for-one exchange. When it comes to funding your next mini-retirement, cash is the easiest starting point.

Bucket 3. Hourly work

Hourly work could look like a part-time job, side hustle, gig economy or freelancing. No matter if you work for yourself, work remotely, babysit, or take a part-time job, what defines hourly work is that you are compensated proportionately for the time you put in.

Like your cash bucket, the great thing about hourly work is

that it's easy to get started. You can apply for a weekend job or see if friends need help with childcare or housework. You could be earning money by this weekend.

Even freelancing isn't terribly difficult to get started with. You will work some low-paying gigs to start. But as your skill, portfolio, and quality client list grows, your income grows with it. I've seen people learn a skill in a month and start freelancing.

If you add just five hours of work a week, 40 weeks out of the year, for $20 an hour, that will give you $12,000 in three years. For someone in their 20s with low expenses, that alone could pay for an incredible adventure during one to two months off. You can funnel extra income into the cash, investment, or debt paydown buckets.

For some people with really high earning potential, it can make sense to focus on your professional growth in your 20s. If you love your career field, I would look for consulting or side work that continues to build your résumé. Often, you can make a much higher hourly rate as a contractor because you aren't being compensated with healthcare, 401(k) matches, and other costly benefits. This is a perfect way to grow your income alongside a 9–5 job.

If you were like me, where work income had a cap, and I wasn't passionate about it, a side hustle in something better paying or more interesting can help not only increase your income but provide a meaningful outlet.

I know lots of people who slowly cultivated interesting and exciting side hustles while they were busy filling their other buckets, like investments, real estate, and reducing debt. As their financial freedom grew, they could make this side hustle that they enjoyed more the main source of income.

Adding some part-time hourly work creates a double win. If you find or create a job, you might be able to do part-time work during your mini-retirement. That income helps you cash-flow your time away from the 9–5. Plus, if you're nervous about finding another job when you finish your mini-retirement, you know you can still create income this way.

Bucket 4. Build a business

I separate business from hourly work by the fact it keeps producing income even when you are gone. This would also include some of the things we refer to as "passive income." For example, I coach and teach, which I get paid for hourly. It is flexible and remote, but if I stop coaching for a few months, I stop creating income from it. But I also have a book and courses. Even if I take a few months off, people can still buy those products while I'm hiking across the southwest. I don't have to log any additional hours for those to create income.

Building a business could be something very involved, like running a coffee shop. It could also be something you aren't as involved in, like owning storage units. Either way, if you leave, it keeps running. Maybe you have staff that allows that to happen, maybe it's more passive.

The most important factor, if you want to build up this bucket, is creating or finding a business that can run without you. If you are needed, you're basically an hourly worker and have built yourself a job. Which is a great bucket to have, but they aren't the same thing.

Thinking through the vision you had for your life from the first two steps in this book, what business fits into that life you were imagining? Businesses take time to build and become profitable, so this isn't a bucket like the cash bucket that will provide mini-retirement funds right away. That gives you time to think through it and explore different options.

Your business doesn't have to be massively profitable to be a powerful mini-retirement bucket. I think most people can build a $50–100k a year business if they give themselves enough runway (five to ten years). But even $1,000 a month is an incredible bucket for mini-retirements. If you want to take a six-month mini-retirement every three years, a thousand dollars a month gives you $36,000 plus the $6,000 while you are on your mini-retirement. Just that modest amount coming from one bucket could set you up for a few incredible mini-retirements every decade.

Bucket 5. Rentals and house hacking

Adam and I were living in a tower apartment near the Pentagon outside of D.C. when I found out our rent was going to go up by 10% year after year. The apartment was under new management, which was in a hurry to maximize its cash flow. I did the math and realized it wouldn't be long before the apartment was out of our budget.

It only made matters worse that the two-bedroom, 800-square-foot apartment was feeling a bit tight after we adopted our oldest son, who was 12 at the time. We had started thinking about having a baby, so moving seemed like the right move. Except that Northern Virginia isn't cheap. Even expanding our search into neighborhoods further from work, house rental prices were 50% more than we were paying.

Then I found the perfect house—well, the perfect price. The house itself looked good on paper: four bedrooms and two bathrooms, a small garage, and a big yard. There were a few oddities, like no dishwasher; instead, the washing machine was next to the refrigerator. And the dryer was out in that small garage that was only accessible by the manually lifted garage door.

I negotiated the price down by $100 a month and locked in a three-year lease. It would still be slightly above our old rent. Even though we were in our mid-20s with a teenager and hopefully a baby soon, we decided to get a housemate. He paid $800 a month, and over the three years we lived there, that one choice helped save us over $25,000.

House hacking is a term that means you make unconventional living arrangements to help keep your housing costs low or to zero. That might be renting a room or two in your place long term or short term, like Airbnb. One friend of mine bought a duplex, and the rent from one side pays almost the whole mortgage and insurance, allowing them to live rent-free. One summer, during the high tourist season, they moved into their RV and rented their side on Airbnb for $200+ a night.

House hacking not only helps fill up your cash bucket before your mini-retirement, but provides you cash flow during your mini-retirement. And if you plan to travel during your time off, a housemate is like a built-in housesitter while you're gone.

After ten years of renting, we bought our first home. We opted for just about the ugliest home we saw, and slowly figured out how to renovate it ourselves. We had enough cash left over to buy our first rental. Adam took a six-month mini-retirement and focused on the remodels, having some time with our four-year-old, and figuring out what the next professional chapter would look like for him. A few years later, we took another mini-retirement to add another rental and take a much-needed vacation.

Rentals are like businesses. They take quite a bit of upfront time, effort, and money to get going. But once they are working, they just keep humming along, creating income month after month. Our two rentals initially generated $1,000 a month in income after all costs were covered. After a few years of renovations, they now produce $1,500 a month or $18,000 a year.

That number alone isn't massive, but again, when you look at it from a mini-retirement perspective, over three years it could add $54,000 to the cash bucket.

Thinking long term, over the next ten years, having some real estate income, either from house hacking or rentals, could give you massive flexibility and freedom to step away from the 9–5 for a few months or a year or more.

Bonus Bucket. Debt paydown

Debt paydown is a powerful place to put your gap money because it creates a double benefit. First, it reduces your baseline budget. For example, your expenses are $5,000 a month, with $500 going to debt repayment. If you are able to pay off your debt, that's $6,000 less you need to save for your baseline budget for your year-long mini-retirement. Plus, as long as your income doesn't decrease after you pay off your debt, you now have an extra $6,000 a year to add to the other buckets.

Because of its double effect, I've always been cautious to add debt to my life. Because freedom and security are strong motivators for me, I'm hesitant to trade those away for small lifestyle upgrades if I can't pay cash.

It's been a couple of decades in the making, but Chad has built and strengthened all five buckets in his financial life, and it's given him a tremendous amount of freedom and security. One of my favorite book titles is *A Long Obedience in the Same Direction*. It's not quick or easy. It's about having a direction in mind and consistently moving that way.

You can guard the gap by strategically building up one or more of these buckets, to afford longer and more extravagant mini-retirements. Up next, we'll tackle the biggest cost fear for Americans taking a career break: healthcare.

CHAPTER TWENTY

HEALTHCARE (IN THE U.S.)

Cue dramatic music... Dun dun duuun! Whenever I talk about the idea of mini-retirements online, the comments section is filled with *"Cool idea but what about hEaLtHcArE?!?"* I get it, because healthcare is so important to our physical and financial well-being. And it's also expensive, confusing, and stressful. This chapter will be geared specifically towards Americans. In part because our healthcare system seems to create more anxiety than it eases. And when I talk to people from other countries, they mostly have a relaxed and clear understanding of what they would need to do to access healthcare when not employed.

My goal in this chapter is to show that you do, in fact, have a number of different healthcare options. If you plan carefully and think creatively, there are solutions for every length of mini-retirement, spanning one month or three years. There are good options for people who have some health complications, and for people who are very healthy.

That being said, there is a unique mental or emotional hesitation when it comes to spending money on healthcare as Americans. I've seen people have large payments for vehicle loans, credit card debt, and student loans but when it comes to paying more than they're used to for healthcare, there's a lot of resistance. I think it's because we've become accustomed to only paying a part of our healthcare cost and having our employer pay the other part. The idea of paying the full amount feels wasteful. This is an area where we need to think a bit more logically about expenses. Your healthcare will be a budget line item just like all of the other line items, so you have to keep that in perspective. For example, if you're used to paying

$400 a month for your healthcare and now, using COBRA, you'll be paying $1,000 a month, then you're paying $600 more a month. Yes, an extra $600 a month is a lot of money; if you're taking a three-month mini-retirement, in total you're spending an extra $1,800. Depending on the amount of income you're giving up, or the expense of your mini-retirement, in the whole scheme of things $1,800 probably isn't a deal-breaker. It's just another expense you can plan for.

I'll outline nine different healthcare options you have in the U.S., and provide some context for which ones might be appropriate in different situations. My biggest encouragement to you is to take two or three hours and figure out what your best option would be and what the true cost is. Healthcare is an area where I see people make all sorts of assumptions about how much they think it will cost without ever spending an hour doing a quick Google search or asking their HR department what their COBRA cost would be.

> You don't have to choose the *perfect* healthcare plan for your entire mini-retirement. You can rotate through these nine options. If you are taking two years off, maybe you start with COBRA for three months, switch to the exchange for a year, then do part-time employment for the last nine months. You aren't locked into any of these choices. It often makes sense to utilize two or three at different times during a longer mini-retirement.

OPTION 1: STAY ON EMPLOYER HEALTHCARE

If you're planning a shorter mini-retirement, one to three months, and are going to return to your current employer, the first option

I would look into is staying on your current employer's healthcare. Healthcare could be part of your mini-retirement negotiation.

Logistically, there are a number of ways in which it can be done. If your employer is feeling generous and wants to guarantee your return, they might cover their portion and your portion of your healthcare cost while you're gone. One way companies facilitate this is by paying you a small percentage of your current salary and then your portion of your healthcare cost is deducted from that. For example, during your two months off they might continue to pay you 25% of your current salary, deducting your normal healthcare costs and 401(k) contributions from that amount.

This could also be part of a larger give and take; maybe in exchange for them covering 25% of your salary, you forgo part of a yearly bonus or take on an extra work project. When we look at the cost of losing employees versus the cost of maintaining employees, paying part of your salary or covering your healthcare cost could still be a huge financial win for your employer.

OPTION 2: COBRA

COBRA allows you to stay on your same employer healthcare plan for up to 18 months after you separate from your employer. On COBRA, you are responsible for your portion and your employer's portion, plus a small administrative fee. This can be a great option for people who are planning to separate from their employer but go back to another job within 18 months.

While it might not be the cheapest option, COBRA does have a huge advantage in maintaining your medical care continuity. You'll be in the same network, accessing the same doctors, and have the exact same coverage as you did while you were employed. This can be helpful for people who have ongoing medical treatment. Switching to COBRA after you separate can be a seamless transition.

I've had clients with expensive medical conditions or planned medical treatments and COBRA made the most sense. It was coverage that they were comfortable with and entailed no adjustments to their medical care. One of my coaching clients planned a six-to-nine-month mini-retirement to help her recover from some burnout. As a family, they had some planned medical expenses that would occur during this time off. Switching to COBRA was an extra expense they had to budget for, but it made the transition easy and less stressful. Because she had a very in-demand career, she knew as soon as she was ready to go back to work there would be lots of jobs available that would offer full benefits.

OPTION 3: ACA MARKETPLACE

Finding a healthcare plan on the marketplace can be a great solution if you're planning a longer mini-retirement—for example, from six months to two years or more. It can also be a good solution if you are hoping for a cheaper option and don't mind switching healthcare plans. You can find a variety of plans that best fit your needs. Because some of these plans are very state-specific, with each state having some of its own unique rules, and because the rules change frequently, I won't try to outline all of the specifics here. My suggestion is to take two to three hours and do a bit of research as to what plans are available in your state and what the actual cost would be.

> If you are planning for a longer mini-retirement, as your income goes down you might qualify for healthcare subsidies. For longer mini-retirements, this can make your healthcare cost very similar to when you were working, or perhaps even more affordable.

CHAPTER TWENTY

OPTION 4: MEDICAID

Medicaid might be an available option for low earners or those with families. It's worth looking into what the options might be in your state. Of course, in America people will have all sorts of big feelings about folks using Medicaid because we have made healthcare so political. So, using Medicaid might be a matter of personal conviction. At the end of the day, it's important for you and your family to have good access to healthcare. If you're planning a longer mini-retirement—say to go back to school for a few years and train for a new career—this might be a helpful option.

OPTION 5: PART-TIME WORK

> Sometimes, you don't need emptiness. Instead, you need a change of pace, which could involve paid work. Imagine for a minute a stressed-out corporate employee. They have so many responsibilities on their shoulders. The work involves meetings, deadlines, managing employees, and hitting targets. Most nights, they send work emails from bed at 11 p.m. They never get a vacation. But perhaps, like me, they have a love of gardening and plants. They want to be outside, walk around, and see the flowers. For that person, leaving corporate life for six months to work at a plant nursery might be a dream. Every day they are outside walking around, watering plants, and—my favorite activity of all—talking to people about plants. The only work they bring home at night is a few plants they bought with their employee discount.

Part-time work can help solve healthcare concerns. This can be a good choice if you're planning for a much longer mini-retirement, where you could use some income as well as healthcare coverage. For example, when people are building a business, they might need two or three years for that business to be able to financially support them. A low-stress part-time job can help fill that gap and build them a longer financial runway.

For some people, working a part-time job would not feel like a mini-retirement and wouldn't give them the outcomes they're hoping for. But if you've been in a very mentally demanding or high-stress environment where you always take your job home, having a chill job at a coffee shop 20 hours a week might sound like heaven.

This can also be an interesting option for married couples. Instead of both partners being completely unemployed, one partner works 20 hours a week. This can provide healthcare for the family, create a bit of income, and open up a tremendous amount of time and flexibility to add new things to your life. If you're planning a longer mini-retirement, say two years, perhaps one partner does part-time work the first year, and then they switch, and the second partner works part time the next year.

OPTION 6: HIGH-DEDUCTIBLE PLAN

A high-deductible plan might be available on the marketplace or offered through your state. One of my clients has a high-deductible plan and only pays $150 a month for his plan. This can be a great option for people who are relatively healthy, have no large planned medical expenses, and don't require much ongoing medical attention. If you have a large emergency fund with the amount of the deductible set aside, there's a good chance you'll come out better financially than by going with a more traditional deductible plan.

For example, if your high-deductible plan saves you $500 a

month versus a traditional plan, and you spend anything less than $6,000 that year out of pocket, you essentially still come out ahead. One of the challenges I do see with this plan is that sometimes it encourages people to not seek out routine healthcare because it is out of pocket. If you go with the high-deductible plan, it's still important to mentally earmark money for your healthcare and seek routine medical care.

OPTION 7: TRAVELER'S INSURANCE

Traveler's insurance can be a great addition if you plan to travel extensively outside of the country during your mini-retirement. Personally, I don't think it should be used as a replacement to traditional health insurance. I've seen people attempt this, and anytime you come back into the U.S. you risk having a medical emergency that won't be covered. That being said, traveler's health insurance is incredibly affordable and can provide some peace of mind while you're traveling.

You can always research the cost of medical care in the country you'll be visiting and weigh the risk versus the cost. In some countries, medical care is very accessible and affordable, so even if you end up with a broken bone or cavity in your tooth, you'll have a very reasonable medical bill.

OPTION 8. HEALTH-SHARING MINISTRIES

Health-sharing ministries aren't exactly insurance, but do help cover your medical expenses. The basic idea is that everyone pays into a large pot of money, and then when members need medical expenses covered it comes out of that same pot of money. These organizations usually have some sort of religious requirement. It could be as simple as checking a box indicating that you're a person of faith, or as complicated as needing a letter from your pastor that you regularly attend services.

The benefit to health-sharing ministries is that they are usually reasonably affordable. Coverage can run anywhere from $200 for a single person to $600 a month for a family. There is a bit more paperwork and a system to learn when it comes to getting reimbursed for your healthcare costs. But most people I talk to say it's not overwhelmingly difficult once you get the hang of it.

My one caution would be to pay careful attention to what is covered and what is excluded from your healthcare coverage. Because there's some religious affiliation, there often can be exclusions to the policy that you might not expect. For example, a friend of mine used a health-sharing ministry for years and really enjoyed her coverage and experience with them. When she started thinking about having a baby, she realized that fertility treatments were not covered in her policy. This wasn't a huge issue, as fertility treatments are frequently not covered in the U.S. The strange exclusion, though, was that if she became pregnant via fertility treatments, they wouldn't cover any of her normal pregnancy-related expenses. For the life of me I can't figure out what the justification for that would be or the logic behind it. Nevertheless, I would look into it to see if there are any odd exclusions to your policy.

OPTION 9. PARTNER WORKS

Perhaps the easiest solution, if you're part of a married couple, is for your partner to continue to work while you take a mini-retirement and stay on their health insurance. This can have a number of benefits, from the continuation of income to not having to stress about changes in your healthcare. But it doesn't all have to be one person having fun while the other toils away. One of my clients planned a three-month mini-retirement over the summer in order to go on a long hiking trip and visit some friends in Europe. His wife would stay employed and provide healthcare for the couple. She would be using all of her vacation time over the summer and requesting some unpaid time off to join him in these adventures. With approaches like this you get the benefit of healthcare with predictable income while still enjoying a lot of the upsides of mini-retirement.

While the U.S. healthcare system can feel daunting, I hope this chapter shows that healthcare is a solvable problem like any other solvable problem. There are several solutions, and you have the flexibility to combine and change things as you go.

STEP FOUR

NAVIGATING THE MINI-RETIREMENT JOURNEY

CHAPTER TWENTY-ONE

PREPARE FOR THE UNEXPECTED

IN THE SPRING of 1804, Lewis and Clark were commissioned by the U.S. government to lead an expedition of men towards the Pacific Ocean. The government had hopes of finding a direct route for commerce and creating maps of this newly purchased land. While it was uncharted and largely unknown to most Americans, it *had* been explored. Native Americans and trappers had experience and expertise in navigating it. In your mini-retirement journey, I'm here to help guide you. It's tough to go places you have never gone without a map. You don't know what lies ahead: the perils or the beauty. While mini-retirements aren't familiar to most, there are people who have taken the journey before you.

Step Four is the road map into unfamiliar territory. In Step One, I highlighted all the amazing points on the map. I showed you where to stop for the must-see attractions. Steps Two and Three helped prepare for the journey, handling the logistics. Now it's time for a heads-up on the challenges you might face and how to easily navigate them. Knowing what is up ahead and how to maneuver will take you from an OK mini-retirement to a life-changing one.

Outside of my online audience and clients, I also get the joy of meeting other people who have embarked on mini-retirements at events or conferences. Half the time, they share with excitement how amazing and life-changing their mini-retirement was. The other half approaches the conversation with more hesitation. They didn't have a map. No one gave them a heads-up on what challenges they might face. So, occasionally, those stumbling blocks became roadblocks. They were left feeling like the mini-retirement was OK, but knowing it didn't reach its full potential.

The problems we face are never the ones we worry about. It wasn't healthcare that fell through. They had no problem finding another job. The budget was great and actually more affordable than they imagined. So why was the mini-retirement lackluster? They experienced common challenges but had no idea how to resolve them. They didn't have a Sacagawea to help them navigate this journey to places they had never gone. Taking the experience from my dozen mini-retirements and hundreds of people I've talked to, here are the ten things you need to traverse this journey successfully.

1. STUCK AT SIX

The idea of taking a mini-retirement is exciting. Full of possibility. But the very first obstacle you might face is fear. Perhaps just a smidge. Perhaps a whole pile of it. Change is always a little scary. And a mini-retirement might be outside of your comfort zone. And, by definition, if you are outside of your comfort zone, you will be uncomfortable.

Six is a sticky place to be. On a scale of one to ten, six is the most sticky. Maybe life is OK. Work is OK. Your marriage, your health, your family, your friendships; they are OK. They are a six. At six, there isn't an enormous upside if you make a change. But the downside feels very real. At six, things can definitely get worse. A mini-retirement means all those areas of your life could possibly improve, but that's hardly guaranteed. You might start talking yourself out of this incredible adventure you dreamed up in Step One. Life isn't so bad at a six. Why be greedy and hope for an eight or nine? A six is fine.

Except when you're 85 and looking back at your life. Then you feel the sinking regret that instead of being bold and chasing after your dreams because they were a little scary, you settled for mediocrity in every area that mattered to you. Looking back from that vantage

CHAPTER TWENTY-ONE

point, the hassle and fear of a mini-retirement are insignificant compared to the benefits. In the rearview mirror, the fear fades. And the meaning and joy of those experiences is amplified.

Not to brag, but for most of my life I had a tremendous capacity to suffer. Forget six being sticky. I could survive long stretches at a three. A two even. I saw my capacity to suffer, to push through, to keep my head down, as a moral strength. I could stay in bad situations long past the point where it made sense. No matter the physical or emotional pain I felt.

Occasionally a client will explain to me that they are miserable at their job, but they can't give it up because it's a dream job. It might be a dream job, for someone else. But it's clearly not their dream anymore. The other side of the coin of the capacity to suffer is the courage to change.

Sometimes the best gift life can give you is to make things much, much worse. Maybe if life or work becomes a three, you'll find the courage to change. The capacity to suffer and the courage to change are both useful skills, in the right time and place. But the capacity to suffer can keep you stuck in places you should have left long ago.

So, after the excitement of the idea fades, before you even start the journey, there might be a little fear, or a lot of fear. You might rationalize to yourself why you're OK with life just being OK. Maybe you'll be proud of your capacity to suffer at a three.

It's a risk either way. Taking a mini-retirement has its risk. But so does everything staying the same. There is a real risk that, at 85, you'll feel regret about the time lost with your kids, opportunities not explored, adventures forsaken, experiences with people you love postponed.

I hope at this point in the book, taking a mini-retirement is the easiest choice you'll make. But if you still feel some fear and hesitation, you're in good company.

2. EXPLAINING TO FRIENDS, FAMILY, AND COWORKERS

When the time comes to finally leave your job and start your mini-retirement, people often have concerns about how they're going to explain this to their friends and family. Adam and I never had issues explaining our shorter mini-retirements, perhaps because one of us was still working. But, when it came time for us to enjoy a full year off together, there were a number of questions and concerns from friends, family, and coworkers. Maybe it was because we had four young children at home and one on the way. Apparently, people with five kids keep jobs, they don't quit jobs. Those closest to us seemed to have a number of concerns, some of which were voiced while others were felt in long, awkward pauses in conversation.

When I coach clients, I hear their fears and concerns about what their friends and family might say or think. Here are some of the concerns that I've heard over the years.

- Your family could be concerned about your future job prospects or worried about your finances.
- If your parents are very hardworking and raised you to be the same, they might judge you as lazy.
- If your family sacrificed so much to give you more opportunities or education than they had, or they helped send you to college, leaving your career is seen as throwing all of that away. This is especially common with first-generation immigrants whose families moved to a new country to give their children more opportunities.
- Your family might not understand where you're coming from, because they suffered through a career they didn't enjoy; why can't you do the same? The ability to suffer is seen as a moral strength.

- Your family might view you as spoiled or entitled, living out some unrealistic fantasy.
- Perhaps your family has been incredibly proud of your accomplishments and success, and your mini-retirement is seen as giving all of that up. You're worried they will feel disappointed.
- You're worried that friends and family will be too invasive with their questions about things that you either don't want to share or don't know all of the answers to.

Keep it simple

The best explanation is the simple one. Create a one-to-two-sentence explanation of what you're doing. Then, just stick to that script. Often, the simple explanation is enough for most friends or family.

Here are a few examples:

"You know how work has been really intense these last few years? Well, I'm planning on taking a six-month break to rest. I have a pile of house projects to finish up and am planning some vacations that I've had to postpone because of my work schedule. During this time, I will be networking and keeping in touch with my professional friends while I look for a new job."

"I've been at my company for a long time now, and it's time to try something new. I'm taking a short break in between jobs in order to [insert cool adventure]. We've been planning and saving for this for a while and are excited about the opportunity."

"Well, I've enjoyed my career thus far, but I have always been curious if there's something else I would enjoy doing professionally. I'm planning on taking the next year to explore new options and

see if there's something that would be meaningful and enjoyable for the next 20 years."

"Things have been really busy with work the last few years, and with the kids getting older I want to take a break now to be able to do some of the cool adventures that we've always wanted to do with them before they head off to college. We have set some money aside to take a year off and do a big road trip."

These short explanations will give context for your choice and provide enough explanation.

Work culture

American work culture is bananas. And it's not just American by any means. It's all around the globe. The worship and morality of work. Tell your friends at work that you're leaving for the crazy goal of improving your life. A few will be genuinely happy for you. Most will be shocked or confused. And some will be angry. *"How dare you opt out of the system I worship?"* When work contains the entirety of someone's purpose, identity, and value as a human, your leaving work might stir up big feelings for them.

Don't let your coworker confuse you with themselves. They might react with anger because they have a big pile of doubt, fear, or insecurity. They will say, *"**You** should be terrified to leave the security of your job,"* when they mean, *"**I** would be terrified to leave the security of my job."* They will say, *"**You** are going to ruin your career,"* when they mean, *"**I'm** scared that would ruin my career."*

Your coworkers are projecting their emotions and fears onto you in the form of "advice." Just because they are confused about whose situation they are referring to doesn't mean you need to be confused. You can put their emotions right back where they belong, on them. You can say, *"I feel really good about this choice, but I get it wouldn't be the right choice for you."*

Give yourself the gift of being misunderstood

Dealing with others' fear, confusion, or anger can be a stumbling block in your mini-retirement journey, especially if you were hoping your time off would be received with excitement and celebration from those who care about you. In relationships, it's important to have emotional boundaries. A boundary draws a line between your responsibility and other people's responsibility. For example, it's *your* responsibility to know why this mini-retirement is important to you. It's *your* responsibility to know how to best spend your time. And it's *your* responsibility to figure out the finances and the logistics of returning to work. None of these things are your family members' responsibility. However, boundaries are tricky because people often confuse your responsibility with their responsibility.

You're not a telemarketer. Your goal isn't to sell anyone on your life choices. You don't have to persuade them about all of the benefits and why it's the right choice for you. These life choices aren't actually made by a committee; there will be no group vote. They are yours alone to be responsible for. The reality is, your friends and family might not understand why you're doing this. But the great thing is, it's not their job to understand. That's your job.

We often want the support of our friends and family. But support doesn't have to mean that they fully understand or approve of all of your choices. A large percentage of people will only truly see and understand something when it's finished. You can show them the drawings for a house design, but it doesn't fully make sense until the house is built. You can walk them through your business plan, but they won't see it until the business runs successfully. You will chase your tail in circles trying to sell someone on an idea before it's completed. Simply go out and do the thing, and after it goes well, you'll have people come back to you and say, *"Oh, that was really a great idea! I wasn't too sure when you first told me about it. But it turned out really well!"*

One of my personal rules for maintaining emotional boundaries is: **I'll answer any honest question.** But oftentimes, what people are saying isn't an honest question. *"I don't think that's a good idea." "I'm not sure you've thought this through." "This seems like an unnecessary risk."* Those aren't questions. Because it's not my job to sell people on my vision for my life, I don't have to convince them to see what I see. Now if they ask an honest question, which could be *"What are you planning to do with your time off?"* or *"How long are you planning to be away from your career?"* or *"What kinds of jobs would you be interested in after your break?"* I'm happy to answer any of these types of questions. Even if the answer is, *"I'm not entirely sure yet, but I plan to figure that out during my mini-retirement."*

If the conversation keeps heading in an unproductive direction, my last resort is saying, *"I hope you can be happy for my happiness."* Because, at the end of the day, that's the minimum amount of support we can expect from friends and family. There are definitely choices that those closest to me have made that I didn't understand and probably would never agree with. But if they're happy, I can at least be happy for their happiness.

Having walked so many clients through this process, I can say that, with a small amount of preparation, 90% of people's fears are unfounded. Friends and family are generally very excited and supportive of seeing you get to chase down some of your dreams and take good care of yourself. Once a few of their concerns and fears are settled, they will often be your biggest supporters.

CHAPTER TWENTY-ONE

3. HYPER PRODUCTIVE OR NAPPING?

I started working with Sara a few months into her mini-retirement. She reached out because, while there were some things that she had enjoyed about her mini-retirement, she also felt some discontentment. She hadn't been as productive as she expected, and felt like she was wasting time. She was thinking about going back to work sooner rather than later. She struggled with the idea that maybe she was the kind of person who couldn't organize their time outside of a 9–5 job. Maybe a mini-retirement wasn't for her. She worried she was actually kind of a lazy and unproductive person outside of the structure of work.

It's common for people to fall into one of two extremes during the first few months of their mini-retirement. There's the hyper-productive group, and the deep rest group. I want to share what both of these look like, and the benefits of both. Given enough time, both groups sort of meet in the middle. I call it the **new normal**.

What to expect: hyper productive

The hyper-productive group simply transfers all of the energy and momentum they had from their working career into their personal life. Their bodies have been running on adrenaline, cortisol, and caffeine for so long. They are in a heightened state, where everything is busy and rushing, and it feels like survival. Transitioning out of that heightened state takes time, so this is the energy they start their mini-retirement with.

This was definitely our experience when we took a mini-retirement as I was expecting my fifth child. Despite being seven months pregnant, Adam and I dove head first into a kitchen renovation for one of our rentals. We also started making progress on our master bathroom remodel, which we had completely gutted. Intermixed in all of these things was a to-do list a hundred items long that each day we slowly chipped away at. It wasn't until after I gave birth that we started to shift into the new normal, mixing in more restful activities with our productive activities.

There can be some real benefits to this approach. This works great for a very short mini-retirement of one or two months with a packed schedule. Maybe you'll be traveling almost the entire duration of your mini-retirement. You might have a massive list of to-do items that you need to get caught up on. There could be a big project or goal that you want to make some real progress on. This approach works if you're not particularly burned out and you feel like you have a lot of mental and emotional energy to dive into something new.

Even if you're planning a longer mini-retirement, starting with a hyper-productive phase can make sense. You can get caught up and clear away some of that mental clutter from all of the items that you didn't have a chance to get to during your 9–5 job. It will give you a sense of accomplishment.

The biggest thing to be mindful of if you start off your mini-retirement with a hyper-productive phase is that it's simply a phase. When given the opportunity for more rest, and the to-do list winds down, you'll find your schedule slowly adjusting. Perhaps you put in ten to 12 really productive hours every day for your job. At the start of your mini-retirement, you might maintain eight, even ten, of those productive hours a day. But a few weeks or months into your mini-retirement, I see people settle into the new normal. They slow down. This is a good and healthy thing, because your body and mind need that rest. Your body is starting to figure out that you are out of the bad situation, and it has access to rest. It will help slow you down. Your energy and motivation will drop off until your body is fully rested.

CHAPTER TWENTY-ONE

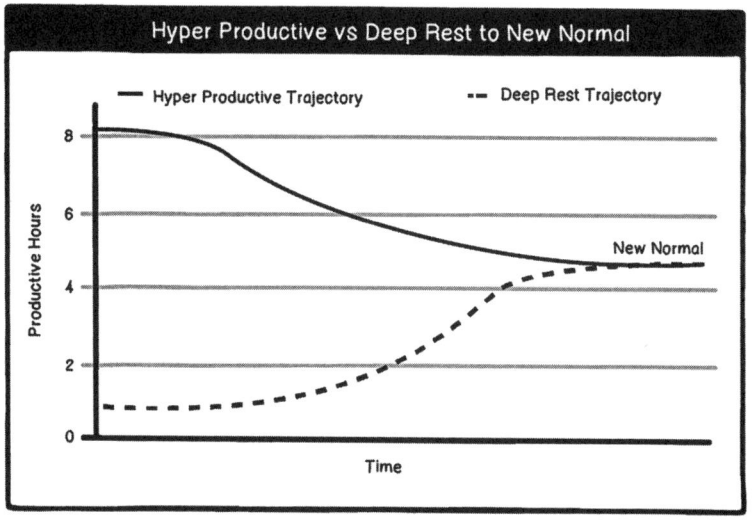

In the new normal, self-care and other personal items start to take more priority. You take some time with your partner in the morning to chat while you drink coffee. You might do a little bit more reading or journaling. You make time to have lunch with a friend. Simple tasks start to expand and take a bit longer. This isn't a bad thing. It's a sign that, instead of pushing through daily tasks in order to get to the next thing, you're enjoying those daily tasks in and of themselves. Cooking dinner isn't a chore that needs to be rushed through and checked off a list. It becomes a nice way to spend 30 minutes. You can get into the new normal phase faster by practicing the **unrushing technique, where you take one activity, like cooking, and practice doing it in a slow and relaxed way**. In the new normal, people often settle into about three to six really productive hours a day. The other hours of the day aren't empty and spent staring off into space. They get filled with exercise, hobbies, relationships, and leisure activities. When people get to this phase in traditional retirement, you often hear them say, *"I don't know how I even had time for a job; my life is so full now."*

Deep rest

You might anticipate you'll go into your mini-retirement in hyper-productive mode. It can be a little discouraging if, instead, you find yourself in what I call a **deep rest** phase. Deep rest happens when you've been running on empty for years—or decades. You've experienced significant burnout mentally, physically, and emotionally. You've pushed your body and your mind past what they were really capable of sustaining for a very long time. Often, people who are severely burned out don't even necessarily self-identify as experiencing burnout. They have felt this way for so long, and they've pushed through these feelings so frequently, that they assume that's life. They've forgotten what it even feels like to feel deeply rested.

The trouble people run into with being in the deep rest phase comes from inaccurate expectations coupled with an inflexible plan. If your expectation was that you were going to be able to be hyper productive, it can be extremely disappointing to find that you actually don't feel like doing much of anything at all. Your motivation and energy drop. There can be a deep "settling in" feeling, like your body is doing a giant exhale. You've shifted into low gear, and no amount of pep talks or shame can kick you back into high gear. Your body simply won't let you take it back to an unhealthy situation.

Then, you start telling a story to make sense of this situation. Just like my client, Sara, people interpret the state of deep rest and giving your body what it truly needs as some sort of character flaw. They worry that that means they are inherently disorganized, lazy, or unproductive. They assume that the only way they can make progress in life is within the structure of a 9–5 job. None of that is true. Your body simply knows it needs rest; it saw an opportunity and seized it.

The reality is that you will probably be in this state of deep rest for longer than you think it should take. A month is the best-case scenario, but I've seen it take two years or longer before people feel totally energized, excited, and motivated to start new challenging projects.

There are three things you can do to mentally support yourself if you are in the deep rest phase.

First, be **flexible**. As you look back to your Step One ideas, can you build some flexibility into the first few months? If you are traveling, give yourself more time or the ability to adjust the itinerary. Save commitments for the middle or end of your time off.

Secondly, **check in** with yourself. Be curious, observant, and non-judgmental about how you are feeling. Check in each day or a few times a day. Are you tired? Do you feel overwhelmed? Do you want to rest? Is your day feeling too full? Ask yourself what you need, and pay attention to the answers.

Finally, **tell yourself better stories**. Don't be judgmental or critical of yourself, asking *"Why can't I motivate myself? Am I really this lazy and unproductive?"* Instead, in a curious, observant, and non-judgment fashion, say, *"Wow, I'm more tired than expected. My body must really want some rest today. Let's move some things around to accommodate that need."*

4. A MESSY KITCHEN

When Adam and I both had 9–5 jobs, occasionally we didn't have the time or energy to clean our kitchen after dinner, so we left the mess for the morning. In the morning, I rushed out the door and left it until that night. The great thing about being at work was I didn't have to look at the mess all day. It's almost like it didn't exist. There were no reminders when I went to prepare a cup of tea in the breakroom. Ignoring a mess is easy when you don't have to look at it.

When you start your mini-retirement, you might find a mess or two in your life you have been successfully ignoring. A demanding career requires a lot of your time and attention. Naturally, this leaves less time and attention for other areas of your life, no matter how important they are. Here are some common ones I've heard and had clients experience.

- **Marital conflict.** There are a number of weak spots in relationships that are easily ignored when people have very little time together. A mini-retirement can provide lots of quality time for a relationship but also reveal some cracks in the foundations.
- **Old hurts.** I see so many people in their 30s and 40s trying to outrun past pain. They work constantly and fill their life with obligations; it's like they are running from an avalanche. Never slow down, and you'll be OK. The trouble with trying to run that fast for that long is you get tired; you burn out. A mini-retirement can provide the needed rest. But it also gives space for you to feel the feelings you've been pushing down, remember the things you've been trying to forget, and look at the things you've been trying to ignore.
- **Lack of friends and community.** There wasn't much time for friendships in the business of life and work. During your time off, you might discover that you have grown apart from some friends. Many people feel like they have a lot of friends, but out of the work environment, they see a much slimmer community than they imagined.
- **Personal discovery.** It's easy to blame work. Work is why you don't have good habits, spend time on hobbies, never get around to calling your mom, or feel stressed all the time. Once you remove the excuse of work, you are left with you. You'll learn a lot about yourself during this career break, but you might not love everything you discover.

- **Weak relationships.** This seems to be especially common in fathers. They thought they had a really strong relationship with their kids. With more time to spend with their kids, the reality proves a bit different. Maybe their kids aren't as excited to rearrange their lives to make time for dad. Or dad realizes he doesn't know as much about their child's life as he thought. Sometimes, being more hands-on in parenting reveals a skill set isn't as strong as you believed. Either you don't understand the logistics of parenting and constantly feel incompetent, or you lack emotional skills like patience and communication.

I know these things are a hard pill to swallow. In half a page, I might have talked you out of taking a mini-retirement. Before you give up on the idea altogether, consider these two things.

The challenge is the opportunity

First, the **challenge is the opportunity.** The mini-retirement might help you discover some hard truths, but the mini-retirement is the perfect opportunity to repair and rebuild. One of my clients had spent years building a profitable business and was in dire need of a break. A few weeks into his mini-retirement we had a coaching call and he was clearly deflated. Already, he had seen that his relationship with his seven-year-old daughter wasn't as strong as he had thought it was. He was understandably sad about that. But... this mini-retirement was the perfect opportunity to start building that relationship into something strong and magical. He now had the time and energy to go on fun adventures, do puzzles, or play games with her.

Your mini-retirement might reveal some challenges, but it also gives you the amazing opportunity to invest time and energy into your relationships and your personal growth.

Better now than later

Second, these challenges have been there all along. You're just noticing and feeling them now. And **now is a better time to fix them than later.** The kitchen was already messy. Your mini-retirement didn't make the kitchen messy; it just gave you the time to notice. You couldn't hurry off to work and avoid the mess. Right now, you still have the opportunity to repair, heal, and build the life you want. You can ignore it and keep chugging away at work, but if you ignore a problem long enough, it might grow past the point of repair.

It's better to take a mini-retirement and work on your marriage at 32 versus divorce at 53. You could practice your communication, attend a marriage retreat, and start life-planning activities together. It's better to invest in your mental health at 28 than become an alcoholic at 46. During your mini-retirement, you could resolve past trauma, learn coping skills and heal codependency tendencies in therapy. I know you want your mini-retirement to be all rainbows and unicorns, and it might be. But if you discover some challenges as well, you have the opportunity to do something about it now versus later.

5. CHECK-IN MEETINGS

In Step One, you created a framework for what you will prioritize and how you'll organize your time. You might notice you didn't create a hyper-detailed step-by-step plan. There is a reason for that. Before you start your mini-retirement, you only know 70% of the information. As you start your time off, you will learn a lot of new information. You'll learn things about yourself, see how the days and weeks are unfolding, and the people around you. If you make a very detailed plan, with only 70% of the information, then 30% of the plan is make-believe. The trouble is people get very emotionally attached to this partly make-believe plan, and when things don't go exactly like they imagined, it can be stressful.

You start with this framework of a plan, and then as you progress through your mini-retirement, you hold **check-in meetings**. Do you remember learning about the scientific method in school? Don't worry if not; this isn't real science, just a half-baked metaphor. The scientific method is the process where you propose a question, make a hypothesis, test the hypothesis, observe the results then iterate. The question is, how do you structure your days and weeks so you can achieve your three big intentions for your time off? All those fun ideas of how this time off would look is your hypothesis. Each week is your experiment.

You are testing out that hypothesis that was based on 70% facts and 30% make-believe. Your check-in meeting is where you will gather all the new information you learned during the week. You'll replace some of the make-believe with new, real information and iterate on your plan. Then, next week, you re-rerun the experiment. Week after week, you observe and learn more, slowly improving the plan.

Consistent check-in meetings are the best tool for keeping your mini-retirement on track. These can be done solo, with your spouse, a friend, or a coach. As you progress through your time off, things will change quickly, and it's important to have the opportunity to reflect on what you're observing and learning. Then, use that information to make small pivots going forward.

Many people feel that their plans get off track or time starts slipping away. Your check-in meeting gives you the chance to course correct. Aim to stay curious and observant, not judgmental. Make sure the language you use reflects that.

How to create a check-in meeting

It can be weekly, biweekly, or monthly. I recommend starting with weekly.

You can do this solo, but if you're married, it's really helpful to do an additional one with your spouse, especially if they are still working. Check in with how they are feeling, how things are working for them, how the experience is differing from their expectations. Again, this is not a time for judgment—be curious about their experience.

Depending on how you best process information, you can journal, use a spreadsheet or graph, or talk through prompts.

Give yourself at least 30 minutes.

Make it a set time, and add it to your calendar.

Prompts

Choose the topics that you are concerned about, such as your mini-retirement goals/intentions, financials, next job, relationship dynamics, phases, etc. Then, have a couple of questions for each topic that will allow you to gather new information. You can use the same questions at each check-in meeting.

Goals/Intentions (assuming weekly):

Does my schedule last week reflect my current intention?

Was my goal at the front of my mind this week, or was I distracted by other things?

Am I really leaning in and optimizing for this intention?

In what ways did things go off the rails last week?

Am I setting clear boundaries with other people and protecting my time and energy?

Based on these observations, what are ways that I want to pivot and adjust for next week?

Financials (assuming a monthly check-in):

Over the last month, what has happened with my spending? Earning? Investments? Savings?

Was that what I expected? Was it in the range of my original plans?

How often have feelings of scarcity or financial fear crept in over the last month? Were those based on my calculations being off? Or is it reflective of my relationship with my money?

Based on last month's observations, are there any strategy changes that are needed going forward? Is it time to adjust the plan?

What are helpful money mantras or ideas that can help ground me in reality when fear creeps in?

Next job

Any updates or new information since last month?

How is the job market in my industry trending? Am I seeing job postings that are interesting?

Do I feel good about the amount of time I'm thinking about the next job, networking, and researching? Is now the right time to focus on that?

How am I feeling about the type of work I do? Anything else that I'm feeling curious about? Is there a small or big job pivot that seems interesting? Any steps I can take to investigate that more?

Going into next month, what adjustments to my schedule, networking, or job research need to happen?

Relationship dynamics (I'll focus on spouse and kids, but this could be any type of relationship)

What expectations have arisen from my spouse (spoken or unspoken) until now?

(to spouse) What is different than you were hoping or expecting in terms of how time, energy, and focus are being spent?

(to spouse) Has my time off helped make you aware of any changes you want in your life or schedule? Are there elements of my time off that you would like to incorporate into your routine?

(to spouse) Any concerns around financials or career?

(to spouse) What would you love to see adjust moving forward?

(for you) Do those changes align with or support the intentions of this phase? Give an update on the progress of the intention of this phase.

(to kids) What's the best part of me having more time with you? What would you love to do more of? Anything that you were hoping we would do together? How are the weeks going? Is that what you expected it to look like? If you could be fully in charge of a day, what would we do? Anything you are concerned about? Anything we should do differently next week?

Phases

What was I hoping this phase would look like? How did last week line up with that original vision?

Am I staying curious and observant, or are my thoughts judgmental regarding my original timeline?

What kind of progress was I hoping for? Am I on track?

How am I feeling about how my progress is lining up with my original timeline?

Do I feel I've gotten what I needed/was hoping for out of this phase? If so, how could I start adding in more of the focus of the next phase? What elements of this phase should I keep? Which do I feel finished with?

Things won't go exactly as planned. You'll get distracted, and life will throw unexpected things at you. Before you start, you don't have enough information to make a bulletproof plan. So you start with a framework. Then, each week, as you stay curious and observant, you gather new data. During your check-in meetings, you look at the data and make adjustments with the most up-to-date information you have.

6. SELF DISCOVERY AND MICRO HABITS

So it turns out you loved the idea of learning Spanish way more than sitting down for an hour a day to study Spanish. Such is life. There are things we used to love but don't care for anymore. There are things that you think you will love, but once you try them, you realize you have no interest. And there are things you do enjoy in the very limited time you can give them, but wouldn't appreciate any additional time spent on them. This is true for all of us. A mini-retirement simply gives you the opportunity to learn it for yourself.

A good friend of mine once said, "I had this massive list of things I wanted to do as soon as I retired. But it turns out that, even with unlimited time, I still didn't want to clean out the garage. I had no interest in doing half the stuff on that list. I gave up a good-paying job to feel guilty for not doing the things I used to claim I had no time for."

Now, you can learn this now, during a three-month mini-retirement, or you can learn this at 65 with a couple of decades stretching out before you. The great thing about retiring often is you can do something about it.

The other challenge with testing hobbies and activities is that you might start as a beginner. In your career, you're good at what

CHAPTER TWENTY-ONE

you do. You're efficient, competent, and successful. Not so with a new hobby or volunteer role. It's awkward, frustrating, and often slow going. That's true no matter when you retire. By retiring often, each time you can up your game. My friend, Chad, is married to a Spanish teacher. They spend their mini-retirements in Spanish-speaking countries. Each time he lives abroad, it's a chance to focus on improving his Spanish skills and watch his kids outpace him as their fluency grows.

One way to prepare for your mini-retirement is to create a list of things you want to start doing on your mini-retirement and **find the micro versions** of those things. Is there a one-minute version you could start doing now? Micro habits have two benefits. They either create a foundation that you can expand upon during your mini-retirement or they help reveal why you are struggling to build that habit. It will show you what things you have resistance around, and help you work through that before you start your mini-retirement. I had a client who planned to start doing yoga every day during her mini-retirement. So, I had her experiment with doing one minute of yoga a day. Every day, she struggled to do it, week after week, proving that lack of time wasn't the challenge. She was then able to discover the real reason why she was struggling to build that habit and problem solve it before she started her mini-retirement.

Your micro habits will give you a good foundation to build on and expand from once you start your mini-retirement. It will spread out the realization that there are some things you are resistant to or don't really want to do. By the time you start your mini-retirement, you'll be able to hit the ground running with an accurate list of how to spend your time.

7. FEELINGS OF SCARCITY

There is a misconception that how we feel about our money moves in tandem with the numbers on the spreadsheet. Feelings of scarcity can be intense for people in every net worth bracket. I've seen people with $100,000, $500,000, or millions feel true guilt and fear around buying $5 of organic strawberries.

There is a certain subset of the population who not only enjoy earning money but really get a kick out of saving and investing money. They love watching those investments grow. While that is a huge help in creating more financial freedom, it often gets in the way of enjoying the financial freedom they are creating.

Often, people have never had to confront their full feelings of scarcity. Earning and saving money dulled the voices of panic and fear. During your mini-retirement, you might not be earning money. You will be spending money. And you might be pulling money from your investments. For people who struggle with feelings of scarcity, this is already uncomfortable. It's like driving down the highway at 75 mph and popping the car into reverse.

There can be a temptation to go barebones on their budget. Now, I believe there is a mini-retirement for almost every budget, so I'm not saying you can't do this affordably. I'm looking at the person with $500,000 in their retirement account and $100,000 in cash who hesitates to spend $150 on an art class.

With no money coming in and lots of money going out, you might want to cut the budget even when the bank account says, *"You're fine! We've got this!"* Let me offer you a different perspective. For most people, the largest single cost of the mini-retirement is lost wages. If you earn $75,000 a year and leave for a year, that time costs you $75,000. You've already paid for it. Now, you might as well spend the extra $150 on the art class so you can truly enjoy the time. It would be like spending $10,000 on an airfare to Paris and $3,000 on the hotel, then being so stressed about the $13,000 you just spent that you skip all the sights so you can save the $15 museum ticket cost. You waste the whole trip stuck in your room eating granola bars, so you don't have to spend $6 on a crepe. You have already paid for the most expensive part of the trip; allow yourself to enjoy the Mona Lisa.

This is why we planned the budget in Step Three. When you feel the discomfort of spending a little extra money while unemployed, take a breath, look over the budget, and remind yourself this was the plan all along. Tell yourself, *"I saved this money with the purpose of giving me more security, freedom, and options. Now it gets to fulfill its purpose."*

8. NOT HAVING A SUPPORT SYSTEM

One of the advantages (and there aren't many) of retiring at 65 is that all your friends and peers are also retiring. All the challenges we face in mini-retirement are still there because you have to figure them out eventually. But at least you're not alone. You can go out to coffee with your friends and complain about fighting with your spouse, bemoan how you're too busy with hobbies, and admit you don't enjoy golf anymore. They will sympathize and offer some advice. They will share their similar experiences. It's a weird transition in life, but you're in it together.

Not so when you retire often. You are retiring alone. None of your friends are joining you in navigating this new life for the next few months.

Take your friend out to coffee who is totally burned out, working 60 hours a week, and has barely slept because of a toddler who wakes up at 4:30 a.m. in the morning. Tell them how you feel lazy because you nap too much. You now have too much time with your spouse and are irritating each other. Or you have so much time for hobbies but aren't finding them as interesting as you hoped. You may have an incredibly empathic friend. Or, more likely, you will hear, *"Are you kidding me right now? Are you complaining about your six-month vacation?"*

Where do we find people who understand what we are trying to figure out? Most likely, it will be in online groups and at in-person events or conferences. One of the biggest benefits of my mini-retirement group coaching is that clients can talk with other people with the same motivations, goals, and challenges. As mini-retirements become the norm and more and more people take them, you might find people locally who would love to hang out, share a beer, and talk all things mini-retirement. One thing people love about my podcast is that they hear all sorts of mini-retirement stories. They know what to expect and how real people handle challenges. You might feel like the only person experiencing this, but your challenge is more common than you realize.

I wouldn't write off your current friends and family group. To the right people, you could say, *"I'm about to embark on this whole new experience. I'm excited but also nervous. I imagine there will be some unexpected challenges. I know you have never done this either, but would it be OK if I share some of what I'm experiencing along the way? They might sound like the most unrelatable challenges, but they are still challenges I'm not sure how to navigate. And I'd love your advice."*

9. BOUNDARIES AND EXPECTATIONS

You've finally started your mini-retirement! You have a great plan for what it will look like. Then, your friend asks if you can help build a deck this weekend. Or your sister wants you to babysit her kids. Your friend decides she can stop over every morning for coffee. Your dad wants to chat on the phone for half an hour a day. Your spouse is irritated that you aren't making dinner.

Before you begin your time off, it's important to have conversations about your intentions and how you plan on structuring your time to accomplish those things. Here are a few common scenarios.

- **Unknown expectations.** Even with clear and honest conversations, expectations will arise after the fact. There are expectations that your spouse will have that they didn't even know they had. They didn't know they would expect you to book all the kids' doctor appointments but now, in the moment, those feelings are surfacing. This is why you need weekly check-in meetings. You don't want these to come out sideways while you're trying to get the kids to bed.
- **Other's entitlement to your free time.** *"Well, now that you have more time…"* Friends and family know that you have more free time on your hands, and they are happy to help you fill it up with their projects or activities. This can be wonderful and a big part of the reason you wanted to take a mini-retirement. But it might be so much that you feel like you aren't making progress on your big three goals. In your check-in meetings, observe and be honest with yourself if others' expectations are derailing your goals. Then it's time to create some boundaries. Maybe you can do x, but not y and z.
- **Spousal envy.** Sometimes, in loving and supportive relationships, one spouse is really good at giving the other spouse the thing they actually want and need. Does your spouse need rest, fun, or self-care? Great, they will help make sure you have that! Because they need it, they can have so much empathy for your needs and prioritize making this mini-retirement happen for you. They are happy in theory. But watching you get the thing they desire can create some feelings of envy. That's totally normal and healthy.

In the weekly check-in, try to pinpoint exactly what your spouse is craving and help figure out how to make that happen for them even though they are still working. It's usually small things: a long bike ride, lunch with a friend, getting two hours to read. Just two to three hours towards what they are craving can go a long way to making this time beneficial for both of you.

Work isn't dictating your time while on your mini-retirement, so it can take extra communication and boundaries with the people you love so that others don't fill your calendar for you.

10. LIFE REIMAGINED

It might be unexpected or even a bit jarring, but one of the most incredible things about mini-retirements is that they give you a chance to **reimagine your life**.

Growing up, I played high-school basketball; I learned how easy it is to get stuck in a mindset or story. No matter if we were ahead or behind in the game, we would start to feel that we were set on that trajectory. If we were struggling to get ahead, it was easy to think we would fail to get ahead the whole game. Discouragement and fear crept in. If we were ahead, it was easy to think that we'd got this and become complacent because we assumed victory was guaranteed.

That's the reason time outs are so important in sports and life. They provide an opportunity to regroup, refocus, and reimagine what needs to happen going forward. I remember many half-time talks in the locker room. During that half-time, our coach would try to snap us out of the old story and help us reimagine what the second half could look like.

Sometimes it worked. We would walk into the locker room behind, having struggled the whole first half, scared and frustrated

CHAPTER TWENTY-ONE

that we might struggle the whole second half. He would paint a picture of how we could turn things around and make the second half a whole new experience. We could pull out the stops with a few good plays, get ahead, and the other team could scramble the rest of the game. Have you ever been to a game where your team was behind the whole time and then, in a very short time, pulled ahead? The energy in the room and players shift. The players and fans are delighted and amazed, and all of a sudden they are on this brand-new path toward victory. It's exhilarating for everyone.

Your mini-retirement might be the very best half-time pep talk you've ever had. In this very short career break, you imagine your career and life moving in a new direction. You have a new vision. A new energy and excitement. And you're not going back to that old energy and old story. Something has changed: your perspective—you.

One of the questions I love asking guests on my podcast who've done mini-retirements is *"Was there any transformation during your mini-retirement?"* Because there almost always is. The perspective and story shifted. It nudged them onto a new trajectory. For some, it's in their health, relationships, personal growth, or career. And the second half of their game will be substantially different than the first. You know it's different; everything in you feels it's different, and anyone watching can tell it's different. There is no way to come from behind, create a big lead, and still feel stuck in a discouraged or frustrated place. You move forward with this whole new energy.

A common theme is that they took a mini-retirement thinking this would be a fun, one-time adventure. By the end, they knew life would be different going forward. They came back and changed their business, decluttered their home, simplified their life, or started creating new income sources. They shifted whatever needed shifting for this to be the new system. The idea of another 20 years of non-stop work followed by a 20-year retirement felt like an absurd notion. Once you see it, you can't unsee it.

RETIRE OFTEN

This is the last thing to watch out for that you might not expect on this journey. You might reimagine your life during the time out. You might pull ahead in some areas of your life. You've set yourself on a whole new trajectory. Life won't ever be the same again. You'll fight like hell to keep that momentum, and no one will steal it from you. Because once you're ahead and winning, you just want to keep winning.

ACKNOWLEDGMENTS

ADMITTEDLY, WRITING A BOOK is a solo activity. But the journey from a childhood dream to its arrival in your hands involves a whole host of characters.

While each character deserves recognition and appreciation, there is perhaps a larger point to be made. If you want to follow your ambitious and outrageous dreams, you'll experience dysregulation, which is like jumping into a pool, barely able to swim. Jumping in the pool is the price of admission. Thrashing about in the pool is terrifying and uncomfortable, an experience that is very close to sheer panic. You need to, somehow, slowly get yourself to the edge of the pool. And hopefully, when you arrive, there will be people cheering you on. People who knew all along that you could do it. Who believed that you were brave and talented and capable. They help you out of the pool and hand you a towel to dry off. Their relentless encouragement enables you to jump back in the pool day after day.

When I was young it was my great grandmother, Doris. There is no single human who could have loved me more than she did. In school, I was terribly shy and dyslexic. While I pondered the universe in my head, on paper, with the numbers and the letters, I didn't do so well. While I seemed like a dim and hopeless student, Mrs. Nelson helped me learn to read every day after school. Slowly, with her help, I memorized the shape of each word until I had the hang of it. In high school, Mrs. J. was never bothered that I couldn't spell simple words. Writing is about ideas and stories and emotion, not grammar or spelling. "There are editors for all that," she would casually say. Mr. Lackner taught me to increase my capacity to suffer when the goal is worthy. Sheer effort could move mountains. And Mr. Melhoff showed me that investing is for everyone, but nearly no one will use calculus.

Those were some of the first people to stand poolside.

How to become a writer in three steps: Write a lot. Share your work a lot. Become friends with other writers. That's about all I know about that. Over the years, Jordan has become my best creative friend, and I might have set this dream aside if we hadn't walked the journey together. JL Collins loved the idea of this book and introduced me to Chris. There are a hundred people I could list out for you. But whatever your dream, you need a few people who have also jumped into that same pool. People who know what it's like to thrash about in there, and know how to get back to the edge. People who think it's a brilliant idea for you to jump in as well. You'll ask them, *"Will this be hard? Or scary?"* And they will say, *"Yes, absolutely, it will! And you should 100% do it. You'll be just fine."*

Years ago, I saw an old friend from school, and the very first thing out of his mouth was, "Well, Jill, I keep expecting to see a book from you on a bestseller list." He said it with such certainty and confidence, the likes of which I have never been able to muster for myself, that I was slightly stunned. I've thought about that one sentence every year since. We need those people poolside as well. Maybe they have no idea how unrealistic their expectations are or how unfounded their hope in us is. But they lend us their unearned confidence. And it softly fans the hope. Over the years, I've kept encouraging cards, printed out blog comments, saved emails from readers. Fans seems an ill-fitting word. We have become friends in this journey together. You all are quite literally the reason the book gets to exist. To the people who have joined me for a month or the

ACKNOWLEDGMENTS

last decade, your presence poolside has made more difference than you will ever know.

And all the people I've shared life with along this journey: Adam, our kids, my mom, Karlie and Marie, the Montana FI Goats, CampFI friends, FinCon community, Joel, Joe and Katie, and dozens of others. And Casey, who basically does all the work in my company and gives me all the credit.

In all the ways I'm rich, my relationships are among the most valuable. This is not to say that these were gifts from the universe. Life provided me a fair share of skeptics, critics, and discouraging people as well. I just didn't give them much space poolside. Poolside spots are reserved for those who relentlessly encourage you to move in the direction of your purpose and goals.

Perhaps the most prominent champion who stood poolside, Chris Parker, my acquiring editor. Your enthusiasm for this book made all the difference. While I thrashed about with fear and neurotic anxiety, you calmly set me back on track. Not only did you help bring the book to market, and substantially improve each page, but your friendship has been dear to me in this journey.

LET'S CONNECT

I HAVE MORE FOR YOU to help on your mini-retirement adventure than could fit into this book. You'll find free worksheets and other resources to help you on your mini-retirement journey at retireoften.com/book.

If you enjoyed the book, I'd love to hear your thoughts. Tag me on social media @jillianjohnsrud. Sharing your mini-retirement stories and experiences is how we can shift the culture, highlighting all the benefits sabbaticals can provide. If you want your story featured, you can connect via retireoften.com/book.

SPEAKING

Interested in having me speak at your event? I love sharing how a mini-retirement can improve your personal life, professional trajectory, and financial freedom.

If your company offers or wants to offer a sabbatical program, I offer keynotes and workshops on why this benefit is so beneficial and how employees can get the most from their time away. Let's connect at retireoften.com/speaking.